Pearson's Canal Comp[anion]
FOUR COUNTIES [RING]

C000110928

Published by Central Waterways Supplies of Rugby, Warwickshire. Tel/fax: 01788 546692.
Copyright: Michael Pearson - All rights reserved. Sixth edition 2000, revised 2002. ISBN 0 907864 86 4 Printed by Graphic Solutions Group.

tillerman

I am reminded of the increasingly popular notice on menus: "All our food is freshly cooked to order. At busy times please be patient." My analogy will be obvious to those who wait as patiently as possible for each new edition of a Canal Companion to emerge. But all our facts are freshly cooked as well, and all the photographs freshly taken, and it is not always easy to judge to the exact month when the stocks of one edition will run out and when a new one will become available. So this is in the nature of an apology to those frustrated boat operators left in the lurch - the moral is, of course, to keep bigger stocks!

And what of the Four Counties Ring? Nineteen years and six editions on from our first essay in guide book publishing its popularity shows no signs of abating. This time we were fortunate to see boats moving on the Caldon Canal too - an almost unprecedented phenomenon in the summer months! Indeed, everywhere we went there were boats on the move, kindly appearing in unison with the sunshine for the benefit of the cameraman. So we hope you approve of this latest 'dish of the day', freshly cooked to our traditional recipe. Just make sure you clean your plate or there will be no seconds!

Michael Pearson

2

High bridge No.57,
Woodseaves Cutting,
Shropshire Union Canal

PRESTON BROOK was formerly one of the North-West's busiest canal junctions. It developed as an inland port where cargoes were transhipped between widebeam Mersey 'flats' and the narrowboats which plied the Trent & Mersey Canal. A substantial number of warehouses were erected to cater for this labour-intensive activity, which continued right up until the end of the Second World War. Indeed, narrowboats traded to and from Preston Brook as late as the 1970s, following which the majority of the warehouses were demolished. The main survivor is the handsome flour warehouse near the northern end of the tunnel.

The actual junction between the Trent & Mersey and Bridgewater canals lies a few yards inside the northern end of Preston Brook Tunnel. It isn't wide enough for narrow boats to pass inside, and access is controlled by a timetable - southbound boats may enter for ten minutes on the half hour; northbound similarly on the hour. Neither is it exactly straight - being one of the earliest canal tunnels it seems that Brindley had yet to perfect the art of digging in a direct line. There is no towpath through the tunnel, so walkers must follow the old horse lane across the top.

At the southern end of the tunnel the Trent & Mersey Company built a stop lock to protect their water supply from being drawn into the Bridgewater Canal. Nearby stands a drydock covered by a valanced canopy which has a distinct railway character. No surprise, for the dock was built by the North Staffordshire Railway - one time owners of the canal - for the maintenance of steam tugs introduced in 1865 to haul boats through the tunnel in the absence of a towpath.

Between Dutton Lock and Bartington Wharf the canal traverses a luxuriant stretch of countryside and there are glimpses to be had of the neighbouring Weaver Navigation, sadly now bereft of commercial shipping.

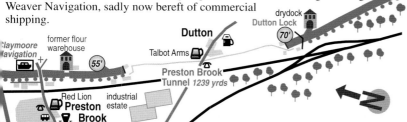

The towpath is mostly wide and flat, though sometimes grassy along this length. Comfortable for walkers, not always so for cyclists!

Summary of Facilities

A post office stores and pub are within easy reach of the canal at Preston Brook whilst the TALBOT ARMS (Tel: 01928 718181) stands above Preston Brook Tunnel.

Three pubs lie close to Bridge 209: THE HORNS (Tel: 01606 852192), the LEIGH ARMS (Tel: 01606 853327) and the HOLLY BUSH (Tel: 01606 853196). Would-be patrons should exercise extreme care, however, as the A49's traffic is fast, furious and unforgiving.

Map labels: Willow Green · Holly Bush · A49 · 207 · pipe · 208 · forge · 209 · The Horns · Leigh Arms · Bartington Wharf · 210 Black Prince · Acton Bridge · By-road to Acton Bridge Rly Sta 1 mile · A49 to Whitchurch · 70' · Dutton Hall · farm shop · 70' · 211 · 212 · 213 · Dutton Locks · Weaver Navigation to Weston Point · drydock · Dutton Lock · Dutton · 70' · Talbot Arms · Preston Brook Tunnel 1239 yds · Claymoore Navigation · former flour warehouse · 55' · Red Lion · Preston Brook · industrial estate · 6 to N. Wales · A56 to Chester · A533 to Runcorn

THE Trent & Mersey revels in its remarkably lovely journey through a rural landscape of rolling farmland interspersed with belts of deciduous woodland, eventually becoming engulfed in the dusky portals of Saltersford and Barnton tunnels. In common with Preston Brook they are just not wide enough to enable narrow boats to pass inside, but on this occasion they are short enough to be negotiated without delay to oncoming traffic. A broad leafy pool, much favoured by fishermen, separates the two tunnels and the old horse-paths continue to provide walkers with a bosky connecting link across the tops.

Of all the so-called "Seven Wonders of the Waterways", ANDERTON LIFT is arguably the most ingenious, and it is unfortunate that it is some twenty years since it last performed its role of raising or lowering craft through the fifty feet disparity in level between the Trent & Mersey Canal and Weaver Navigation. Happily work is now underway to return the structure to full working order, with completion earmarked for late 2001.

In the meantime you can visit an information centre (adjacent to Bridge 199) devoted to the Lift and offering more detail as to its history and operation than we have space to feature here. Briefly, though, it was designed by Edward Leader Williams and opened in 1875, consisting of a massive iron framework

continued on page 7

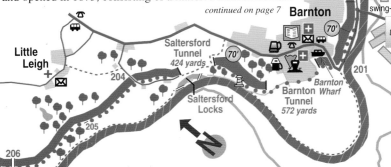

Summary of Facilities

Barnton (best approached from the north portal of Barnton Tunnel) is well served with shops including general stores, a butcher, post office, two chemists and a Chinese takeaway. There is also a useful post office store at Anderton.

There are several pubs along this length, most obviously the STANLEY ARMS (Tel: 01606 75059) opposite Anderton Lift and the SALT BARGE (Tel: 01606 43064) across the road from Lion Salt Works at Bridge 193. THE MOORINGS (Tel: 01606 79789) is located at Anderton Marina and offers lunch and dinner.

Frequent buses run from both Barnton and Anderton to and from Northwich town centre. Tel: 01244 602666.

supporting two water-filled caissons, each of which could carry a pair of narrowboats. Originally hydraulically powered by steam, it was rebuilt early in the twentieth century to electrical operation. Commercial use ceased in the 1960s, but the Lift remained in operation until 1982 when it was closed due to structural faults. Unique in Britain, it has operational cousins in Belgium and France to whom the passage of time has been somewhat kinder.

East of Anderton the Trent & Mersey winds past Marbury Country Park largely untouched by the outskirts of Northwich, though there are occasional glimpses of the town and its chemical industry nestling down in the valley of the Weaver. Centuries of salt production has destabilised the landscape. In 1958 a new length of canal had to be dug at Marston to by-pass a section troubled by subsidence. Lion Salt Works was the last in Britain still producing salt by the process of evaporation in open brine pans. By the mid Eighties it was struggling to compete with more up to date mass production techniques before it finally went out of business - now it is being restored as a working museum, and is usually open to the public for visits between 1.30-4.30pm - Tel 01606 41331 for further details.

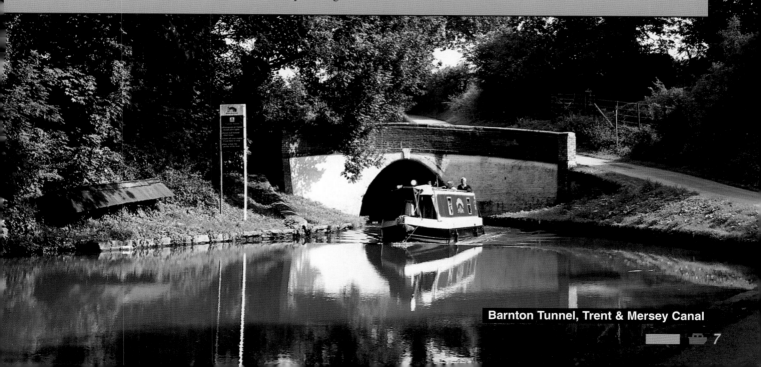

Barnton Tunnel, Trent & Mersey Canal

PREDOMINANTLY rural in character, the Trent & Mersey Canal makes its way through the peaceful valley of the River Dane, only the suburbs of Broken Cross and the ICI works at Lostock contrive to break the bucolic spell. The most curious feature of this section of the canal are the subsidence-induced flashes bordering the main channel to the south of Bridge 181. That nearest the bridge was once filled with the submerged wrecks of abandoned narrowboats, an inland waterway equivalent of Scapa Flow. Many of the boats were brought here and sunk en masse during the Fifties in circumstances almost as controversial in canal terms as the scuttling of the German fleet at Scapa after the First World War. In what was probably a book-keeping exercise, British Waterways rid themselves of surplus narrowboats in a number of watery graves throughout the system. In recent years all the wrecks have been raised and taken off for restoration. One generation's cast-offs become the next's prized possessions. Hereabouts the Dane, nearing journey's end at Northwich where it joins the Weaver, has grown sluggish with age, meandering about its level valley in a succession of broad loops, so that at one moment it is hard by the canal, the next away across the fields of milking herds. The soil here is soft and the river carves deep banks shadowed by alder and willow.

KEEP TO CHANNEL !

176

177

River Dane

Whatcroft Hall

178

179

By-road from Lach Dennis

181

Orchard Marina

A556 from Altrincham

A530 from Middlewich

By-road to Davenham

The Wincham Wharf

Wincham Wharf

189

182A

182

Broken Cross 70'

183

Higher Shurlach

bakery

Northwich - Sandbach (goods only)

Wincham Wharf

lagoons

186

184

Old Broken Cross

185

pipes

ICI Lostock Works

Rudheath

launderette

189

sites of salt works

70'

MANCHESTER

A559 from Altrincham

2

8

A559 to Northwich CHESTER

B5082 to Northwich

River Dane

A556 to Chester

Summary of Facilities

Two attractive pubs punctuate your progress along this length of canal. THE WHARF at Wincham (Tel: 01606 46099) is a warehouse conversion located alongside Bridge 189. In contrast, the OLD BROKEN CROSS (Tel: 01606 40431) by Bridge 184 is a long established, but refurbished, boatmans' inn offering a good range of food.

There are fish & chip and Chinese takeaways west of Bridge 189. West of Bridge 184 you'll find a general store, newsagent, launderette and off licence. Northwich station lies along the same road, approximately a mile from the canal. A large Tesco superstore (open 24 hours) stands alongside the station.

MIDDLEWICH is one of those arcane places well-known in canal circles but meaningless to most other people. In the old days it was salt which brought so much traffic to Middlewich's canals; the salt boats and, of course, the coal boats without which industry could not function in that pre-electric age. Now, though, it's with pleasure boating that this small town is predominantly concerned, with two hire fleets and a boatyard adding traffic to the often frenetically busy Trent & Mersey Canal.

Five locks punctuate the canal's progress around the eastern edge of the town. The central three - deep and tediously slow to use - are bordered by compounds of stacked pallets and the baleful architecture of small industrial units; all a far cry from the salty scenes of the past, when Seddons and Cerebos were at their zenith and a forest of flaring chimney stacks appeared to support the Middlewich sky.

North of the town, Croxton Aqueduct carries the canal over the River Dane, not far from its confluence with the Wheelock. Originally the aqueduct was built to broad-beam dimensions. Close inspection of the undergrowth reveals some remnants of the old supporting piers. Now, ironically, it is just about the narrowest place between Preston Brook and Middlewich.

Big Lock lives up to its name, recalling the original concept that the canal be capable of handling widebeam craft inland from the Mersey ports as far as Middlewich: that, at least, was the idea, until someone decided to skimp on the tunnels.

Five years since our last full survey, Town Wharf was still 'To Let'. Strange and sad how some former canal buildings seem so ripe for redevelopment whilst others are stifled and moribund.

Middlewich Narrowboats' hire base and boatyard, with its old canal managers' house and attractive canopy, strikes a welcome element of dignity. Their drydock was once used by Seddons to maintain their fleet of narrowboats.

Bridge 168 spans what is ostensibly the Shropshire Union Canal's Middlewich Branch, though the first hundred yards were actually built by the Trent & Mersey in a ruse to extract increased tolls. Keep an eye on boat movements here for Middlewich can suddenly become Muddlewich when someone comes shooting out of the Shropshire Union without advance warning. More interesting industries line the canal as it escapes, southwards, from the town, not least the Bisto gravy works!

see page 10 for details of Middlewich facilties

Map labels

chemical works
163
162
161
70'
Booth Lane Locks
28ft 9ins
164
165
Ah Bisto!
salt works
sanitaryware works
Rumps Lock
9ft 2ins
166
Middlewich Locks
32ft 7ins
Kings Lock
11ft 3ins
169
172
Town Wharf
168
Wardle Lock
9ft 9ins
31
Big Lock
5ft 0ins
70'
River Dane
town centre
textile wrks.
Middlewich
30
29
28
173
70'
Croxton Hall
175
Croxton Aqueduct
mill
aqueducts
River Wheelock
Stanthorne Lock
11ft 1in
27
Middlewich Manor
40
A533 to Northwich
A530 to Nantwich
drydock
169
Kings Lock Chandlery
70'
168
167
Middlewich Narrowboats
Andersen Boats
31
DANGER!

9

Middlewich *(Map 4)*

A salt making town since Roman days, Middlewich's most interesting building is the parish church of St Michael whose tower is scarred with missiles unleashed during the Civil War.

BIG LOCK - canalside Big Lock. Good range of beers, bar meals and a la carte menu. Attractive canalside seating area. Tel: 01606 833489.

KINGS LOCK - canalside Kings Lock. Food and accommodation. Tel: 01606 833537.

NEWTON BREWERY INN - canalside south of Big Lock. Old fashioned Marston's local. Tel: 01606 833502.

In the town you'll more Baltis than Bangladesh. BALTI SPICE has the dubious distinction of occupying the once elegant premises of Vernons butchers - Tel: 01606 837030.

Fish & chip shop by Kings Lock.

Old-fashioned shops make this a pleasant town to restock the galley. There's a large Somerfield supermarket nearby, as well as branches of NatWest and Barclays banks. A small market is held each Tuesday, whilst a number of shops close at midday on Wednesdays.

BUSES - frequent services to Crewe, Sandbach etc depart from the Bull Ring. Tel: 01270 505350.

Sandbach *(Map 5)*

Chiefly famous for its ancient Saxon crosses, Sandbach lies about a mile east of the canal at Ettily Heath, though there is easy access to the railway station from Bridge 160. In transport circles Sandbach is lauded as the home of lorry making. Fodens had their roots in 19th century agricultural machinery and they were at the forefront of the development of steam lorries. Edwin Richard Foden (ERF) broke away from the family business to concentrate on diesel lorries and, seeing how successful he became, the family followed suit! You cannot drive very far nowadays without meeting a modern juggernaut built by one or other of these firms.

Wheelock *(Map 5)*

Although by-passed by the A534, Wheelock still endures more than its fair share of traffic - a culture shock after the peace of the canal. Nevertheless, it's a useful pitstop with a newsagent and post office selling canal souvenirs. Refreshment opportunities are plentiful: try the CHESHIRE CHEESE (Tel: 01270 760319), the wonderfully unspoilt COMMERCIAL HOTEL (Tel: 01270 760122), DE VENEZIA (wharfside Italian restaurant), or the fish & chip shop. Buses to Crewe and Sandbach.

Hassall Green *(Map 5)*

Isolated community somewhat impinged upon by the M6. But there are still pleasant walks to be had along country lanes. Downhill, past the mission church painted shocking pink, the old North Staffordshire Railway has been converted into the "Salt Line" bridleway. There's a pottery adjacent to Bridge 146 . Refreshments are available at the LOCKSIDE RESTAURANT (Tel: 01270 762266) or at the ROMPING DONKEY (Tel: 01270 765202), a country pub only a few hundred yards north of Bridge 147. The canalside post office stores stocks a good range of canal souvenirs, books, maps etc. Various boating facilities are also available here.

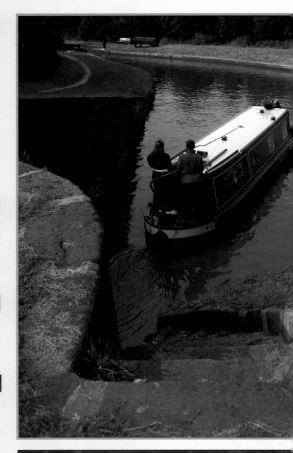

Middlewich Locks, Trent & Mersey Canal

LOCKS proliferate, and are potentially habit-forming, as the Trent & Mersey ascends from (or descends to) the Cheshire Plain. There are twenty-six chambers to negotiate in only seven miles between Wheelock and Hardings Wood, and "Heartbreak Hill" - as this section has been known to generations of boaters - seems an all too appropriate nickname by the time you have reached the top or bottom; 250 feet up or down.

With the exception of the PIERPOINT pair, all the locks were 'duplicated' in the 1830s, paddles between adjoining chambers enabling one lock to act as a mini-reservoir to its neighbour. These side paddles were taken out of use when commercial traffic ceased towards the end of the 1960s, but the duplicated locks still ease delays today, as well as offering the opportunity to exchange travellers' tales with boaters operating adjacent chambers.

The locks may, or may not, make life hard for the boater, but the canal itself is illuminated by a succession of small communities with interesting pasts. Sandbach stays a stubborn mile or more out of reach of the canaller, but you can savour the voyage around its outskirts and intermittent views of the tower of its parish church. At ETTILY HEATH the quadrupled, electrified tracks of the Crewe to Manchester railway cross the canal at the site of a transhipment basin provided to facilitate traffic with the Potteries. Hereabouts the canal, concrete-banked and steel-piled, tends to be deeper than is normal on account of subsidence caused by salt-mining in the past. The River Wheelock rises in the vicinity of Little Moreton Hall and gives its name to a former wharfingering community situated where the Crewe-Sandbach road crossed the canal. MALKIN'S BANK was home to the families of boatmen engaged in comparatively short-haul traffics connected with the salt and chemical industries. They lived cheek-by-jowl with employees at the huge Brunner-Mond sodium carbonate works which is now buried beneath the greens and fairways of Malkins Bank golf course. Between locks 62 and 63, a side bridge carries the towpath over an old arm (now used by a boatbuilder) which once went into the chemical works.

Locks marked 'dup' are duplicated - ie there are chambers side by side and you may use either chamber in either direction, though note that from time to time one chamber may be closed for maintenance.

11

ONE hardly knows where to begin describing this richly rewarding length of the Trent & Mersey Canal as it makes its purposeful way through the long line of 'Cheshire Locks'. All the locks were duplicated under the direction of Thomas Telford in the 1830s, though one or two have since been singled. Most peculiar of all, perhaps, was the rebuilding of one of the THURLWOOD LOCKS in 1958. Subsidence from the adjacent salt works had brought Lock 53 to the brink of collapse, and so a new chamber was designed in the form of a steel tank supported by a series of piers which could be raised should further subsidence occur. Entry to the chamber was through guillotine gates. In practice the steel lock took longer to operate and was mistrusted by boatmen. It had been out of use for many years before demolition in 1987.

Another structure of significance was lost to the canalscape at RODE HEATH where a large warehouse with arched loading bay stood beside the waterway until being controversially demolished in 1981. Hearing that the mill, a local landmark, was to be demolished, the Trent & Mersey

Canal Society successfully applied for the building to be given listed status. In response the mill's owners took the matter up with their local MP who managed to have protected status overturned. "After further consideration," quoted the DoE "we came to the conclusion that the building was not as interesting as at first thought."

LAWTON 'TREBLE' LOCKS are Telford's work and replaced a Brindley staircase which was both time consuming and wasteful of water. Beyond Church Locks there is a brief respite from the locks and the pleasant site of Lawton church at the edge of woods surrounding Lawton Hall. Throughout this length the countryside dips and sweeps away from the canal in folds and creases like a carelessly discarded garment, revealing lush pastures interrupted by pockets of woodland through which footpaths beckon enticingly. Mow Cop (pronounced to rhyme with 'cow') overlooks this delightful landscape from its high ridge, an appropriate platform for the sober, yet lofty ambitions of the Primitive

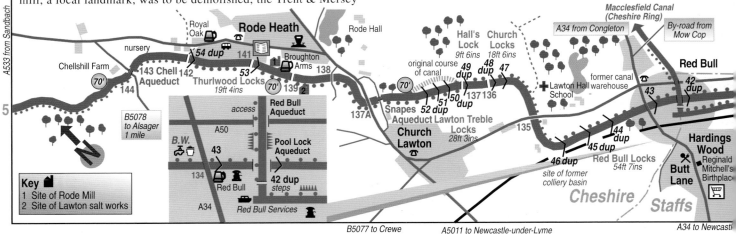

Methodists who held their first open air meeting on its summit in 1807. The castellated ruin, typical of 18th century romantic landscaping, is known as Wilbraham's Folly.

RED BULL LOCKS - once individually known as Townfield, Kent's and Yewtree in order of ascent - are probably the most visually satisfying on the whole of 'Heartbreak Hill'. All the elements are there by happy accident: a long, low stone wall separating the towpath from fields; the sweeping symmetries of the paired chambers masked from the railway by a high bank of beech trees; and an old whitewashed warehouse, once used for the storage of perishable goods, has been refurbished as offices for British Waterways.

POOL LOCK AQUEDUCT seems weighed down by the responsibility of carrying the Macclesfield Canal over the Trent & Mersey. It's not an elegant work of engineering, but it's stood here for 150 years and is no doubt good for a few more. Neither is the upper canal technically the 'Macclesfield', because it was the T&M themselves who built the Hall Green Branch, the Macclesfield Canal proper beginning at Hall Green stop lock one mile to the north beyond a second bridge, the Red Bull Aqueduct, which carries the canal over the A50 trunk road. The Macclesfield Canal is part of the popular "Cheshire Ring" canal circuit featured in another Pearson's Canal Companion and also recognised as a long distance footpath in its own right. Eastbound travellers along the Trent & Mersey, mystified by the Macclesfield's motive for crossing the T&M at this point, should turn to Map 7 for the exciting denouement.

Rode Heath & Thurlwood

Two pubs vie for your custom: the BROUGHTON ARMS (Tel: 01270 765202), canalside by Bridge 139, and the ROYAL OAK (Tel: 01270 875670), reached from Bridge 142. Both are popular with boaters. Shops include a Chinese takeaway (Tel: 01270 873391), off licence and village store/post office. Buses run to The Potteries - Tel: 01270 505350.

Red Bull & Butt Lane

The RED BULL (Tel: 01270 782600) overlooks Lock 43 whilst MRS B'S VICTORIAN SUPPER ROOMS (Tel: 01782 775654), located along the A34 towards Newcastle, are highly recommended. Reginald Mitchell, designer of the Spitfire fighter aeroplane, was born nearby.

Kidsgrove *(Map 7)*

A former colliery town on the wrong side of Harecastle Hill to qualify as a member of that exclusive hell fire club called The Potteries. Its initially foreboding air thaws on closer acquaintance. A path leads up from the tunnel mouth to St Thomas's, "the bargee's church", and there are signposted ways through nearby "Kidswood". James Brindley is buried at Newchapel, a couple of miles to the east.

There are three pubs adjacent to the canal: THE TAVERN (Tel: 01782 775382) and the BLUE BELL (Tel: 01782 771371), both by Lock 41, and the HARECASTLE HOTEL Tel: 01782 773925), close to Bridge 132; the latter serves a good range of meals both sessions, with vegetarian options available.

Kiddy's shops are its strongpoint. They may look dour from the street, but over the counter the natives are at their most vital. Surprisingly, the heart of the town lies not along the main thoroughfare, but on and around Market Street (there is indeed a small market held every Tuesday). Here you will find a KwikSave supermarket, butchers, bakers. Make it your business to find BRENDA'S where you can watch oatcakes and pikelets, those twin bastions of North Staffordshire gastronomy, being freshly made on the griddle, and have your oatcakes crammed with a choice of fillings. Calor gas and solid fuel are obtainable from SMITHSONS by Bridge 132.

BUSES - Frequent services to Hanley and throughout the area. Tel: 01782 207999.
TRAINS - Regular service to/from Longport and Stoke - useful for towpath/tunnel top walkers. Tel: 08457 484950.

Longport *(Map 7)*

All the 'ports' - Long, Middle, West and New - lie down in the valley beside the canal and the origin of their names is obvious, forming as they do, a necklace of wharfingering communities where the import and export of cargoes of The Potteries were handled. Longport, lying as it does on an incredibly busy link road with the A500, makes few concessions in appearance. Lorries thunder through leaving a tidemark halfway up the fronts of shops where merchandising and point of sale are alien jargon. Inside, bare counters display the meagre stocks which constitute essentials, Brand names that have disappeared from more sophisticated shelves eke out a twilight of diminishing trade for their manufacturers. Sweets still come in jars, sausages in links, vegetables in brown paper bags, and service with a penetrating smile of sincerity.

Two pubs stand close to Bridge 126: the PACKHORSE (Tel: 01782 577322) and the DUKE OF BRIDGEWATER (Tel: 01782 790261). The former is CAMRA recommended. Fish & chips from shops either side of Bridge 126.

BUSES - frequent services up the hill to Burslem - Tel: 01782 207999.
TRAINS - infrequent services to/from Stoke, Crewe & Manchester.

AT HARDINGS WOOD the Macclesfield Canal makes a junction with the Trent & Mersey. For eastbound travellers the mysteries of Map 6 are enlightened. If, on the other hand, you have just emerged, still blinking, from Harecastle Tunnel, you may be baffled to find a canal, destined for the north, making its exit to the south. All will be revealed on Map 6.

Taking a boat through Harecastle Tunnel is one of the great inland waterway adventures. At most times there is a tunnel keeper at either end responsible for controlling passage through the narrow bore. You may be delayed waiting for oncoming boats to clear the tunnel before the keeper gives you, and perhaps others going your way, instructions to enter. Gingerly you penetrate the gloom beyond the portal. Gradually all sense of light is lost. Nostalgically you look over your shoulder at the retreating half-moon of daylight. Suddenly, with a shuddering clang, the doors at the southern end close and the fume extractor fans begin to suck with a muted roar. For the next three-quarters of an hour you are buried deep beneath Harecastle Hill: with one small niggle at the back of your mind,

will you or won't you come face to face with the 'Kidsgrove Bogart'?

The original tunnel through Harecastle Hill was designed by James Brindley. It took eleven years to build, was one and three-quarter miles long, and opened in 1777, five years after Brindley's death. A series of connecting tunnels led off the main bore to adjacent coal faces beneath Golden Hill, intersecting with several underground springs which provided additional water supplies to the summit level. A curious feature of this seepage occurs to this day, in that the water either side of the tunnel is tinted a peculiar orange shade by minute particles of ironstone rock.

For fifty years, teams of 'leggers' propelled boats through Brindley's towpathless tunnel, lying on their backs at right angles to the boat and literally 'walking' from one end to another, a feat which took two to three hours depending on the amount of alcohol consumed beforehand. Not surprisingly Harecastle became a serious traffic bottleneck. Reluctantly, being well aware of the costs and difficulties involved, the canal company commissioned a second bore with Thomas Telford as consultant engineer. Some idea of the advances in technology gained in the interim can be gauged from the fact that the new tunnel, equipped with a towpath, was completed in less than three years, opening in 1827.

Until the early years of the 20th century, the two tunnels were used in unison: Brindley's taking southbound boats, Telford's north. In 1914 electric

Kidsgrove

4 Counties

Tesco

132 Town Centre
Kidswood

98 dup
131
97

Harecastle Tunnel North Portal

41 dup
T & M
98
132
"Macc"
HARDINGS WOOD JUNCTION

Gas, diesel, solid fuel

Access to Kidsgrove Town Centre

132

131

w.c.
Tunnel Keeper

Boathorse Road

airshaft
airshaft
Traveller's Camp
airshaft

Ravenscliffe

Harecastle Tunnel South Portal

70'

site of ironworks

Tunnel Keeper

130

A527

129

By-road from Tunstall

128

127

Westport Lake

P

126

Longport Wharf

pottery 126

Pack-horse

Duke of Bridgewater

Railway

A527 from Tunstall B5051 from Bursle

70'

Longpor

126

To A500

A527 to Newcastle-under-Lyr

6

tugs began to haul strings of boats through Telford's tunnel and Brindley's, now riddled with subsidence, was abandoned. The tugs were curious machines, unique on our waterways. They dragged themselves along a steel cable laid on the canal bed, collecting power through a tram-like pole from an overhead cable. They successfully solved Harecastle's traffic flow problems into the 1950s, by which time the number of boats using the tunnel had diminished so as to render them unviable. In 1954 forced ventilation was introduced, enabling powered boats to pass through, a system still in use today. Further subsidence caused closure of the tunnel between 1973-77, but much money has been spent on its rehabilitation and it is now in excellent condition.

Refurbishment of the tunnel involved removal of the towpath, so walkers are faced with the option of catching a local train between Kidsgrove and Longport, or following the old boathorse route across the top, encountering the arcane, unvisited landscape of Harecastle Hill which Brindley and Telford must have been familiar with in their time. It seems little changed, and the chattering magpies which keep you company may quite possibly be re-incarnated navvies. Nearing the hilltop, the lane becomes more potholed, bounded with rough pasture grazed by unkempt ponies, whilst airshafts trace the tunnel's subterranean passage, reminding you that there is a canal down there somewhere. Breathtaking views encompass Jodrell Bank, the Wedgwood monument and the exciting urban panorama of the Potteries. In fact, all things considered, this is an adventure every bit as exciting as the boater's rite of passage underground.

Between Harecastle's southern portal and LONGPORT, the canal runs

Counting them out - Harecastle's southern portal

along its 408ft summit at the foot of a ridge supporting Tunstall, northern most of the six Potteries towns. Industry once thronged the cut, but there is an air of desolation here now. From Bridge 129 to 130 the vast Ravensdale ironworks framed the canal, as massive in its heyday as Shelton Bar, three miles to the south. Today, though, no trace remains at all. Indeed the only action is provided by cars and lorries thundering across the new Tunstall by-pass, completed late in 1998. Nevertheless, for the industrial archaeologist the adrenalin will be flowing. Look out for Copp Lane canal cottages by Bridge 129, the ruined edge of the side bridge which spanned the ironworks arm, and the stubs of old basins where the gasworks stood by Bridge 128.

When Potteries folk lack the fiscal means to reach Rhyl or Blackpool, they come down for the day to Westport Lake where they can indulge in an ice cream cone and promenade the circumference of the lake, reopened after its landscaping by no less a personality than the former Prime Minister, Edward Heath. Good moorings are available here usually with the sense of security engendered by the proximity of fellow boaters. In the vicinity of LONGPORT some of the traditional aspects of North Staffordshire make their presence felt. A fine example of the once ubiquitous bottle kiln looms over the canal by the premises of Price & Kensington, whilst another lies tucked away at the back of Middleport Pottery, where a couple of old cranes hang over the water's edge as if the arrival of the next narrowboat laden with felspar or flint is imminent. Longport Wharf itself remains intact, a typical canalside depot where consignments would be collected and delivered by road transport.

Traditional Potteries factoryscape at Middleport

THE Trent & Mersey Canal plunges through the heart of the manufacturing district it was built primarily to serve. It is a heart, however, broken repeatedly as heavy industry has given way to the microchip. Until 1978 the canal penetrated the torrid core of Shelton Bar steelworks, scene of H.G.Wells' terrifying short story, *The Cone*, in which the steelmaster murders his wife's would-be lover by pushing him into a furnace. For a couple of decades thereafter only a rolling mill remained in use, though canal travellers were required to pass through the gloom of two overhanging fabrication sheds. In the first Spring of the new millennium, however, the plant closed totally, and was slowly being demolished as we researched this edition. No longer will you wave at the shunting engine drivers, no longer will the steelworkers cross the canal on their way back to Burslem at the end of a shift. In time some new development will rise from the rubble, sleek and shimmering and soulless in the extreme.

The derelict acres left behind after demolition of the blast furnaces became the site of the 1986 National Garden Festival, subsequently developed into the Festival Park, a ubiquitous mix of leisure, retail and commercial facilities. Such transformations are not without irony. Centrepiece of Festival Park is a hotel converted from Josiah Wedgwood's original Etruria Hall built on a green-field site contemporary with the canal. During the 19th century the steelworks had encroached on the mansion, gradually engulfing its landscaped grounds. So, in a way, the developments of the 1980s returned the neighbourhood to its origins. Anyone familiar with the canal prior to the shutdown of Shelton Bar, however, is bound to mourn the lost drama associated with navigation through the cacophonous and acrid plant.

Like many heavily industrialised regions, The Potteries have passed through a period of transition; though here, perhaps, the pace of change has been less relentless, and something of the old atmosphere is still tangible. From time to time you come upon examples of the area's most potent symbol, the bottle kiln. There was a time, before the Clean Air Act, when visitors could purchase postcards depicting The Potteries' skyline blackened by the combined emissions from serried ranks of these ovens.

For reasons never convincingly explained, Arnold Bennett - who is to The Potteries as Hardy to Wessex or Lawrence to Nottinghamshire - always referred to just 'Five Towns' in his prolific novels and short stories which portray the area around the turn of the last century. He wrote that the Five Towns could never be described adequately because Dante had lived too soon. Inferno or not, five towns or six, there was always, and still to some extent is, a proud independence and individualism about The Potteries which sets it apart in an island between the Midlands and the North. Notice how the local accent has more in common with Merseyside than Manchester: could this have something to do with the development of the Trent & Mersey and the associations it prospered?

Between MIDDLEPORT and ETRURIA the canal twists and turns frequently, following the contours of the valley of the Fowlea Brook. Near Bridge 125 stands the terracotta gabled end of the Anderton Boat Company's former premises, a well known carrier in the district whose boats were nicknamed 'knobsticks'. Nearby, on a site now occupied by modern housing, stood Newport Pottery, famous for its connections with Clarice Cliff, the celebrated creator of 'Bizarre' and other Art Deco ceramics and pottery designs.

By Bridge 123 an arm once led to Burslem Wharf, scene of the pantechnicon's immersion in Bennett's hilarious novel, *The Card*. The arm was abandoned in 1961 after a breach caused by subsidence but there are currently proposals that it could be reinstated for moorings and leisure use.

Post-industrial wastegrounds waiting to be transformed into business and retail parks border the canal. Here and there are clues to a busier past: a boat dock beneath a roving bridge and another bridge where the 'Loop line' railway once weaved its way from one Six Towns community to the next. A wooden, windlass-operated lift bridge frames entry to the Festival Park Marina where secure moorings are available for an overnight stop and the chance to indulge in all the spurious activities modern life offers: supermarkets, ski slopes, swimming pools with wave machines, ten pin bowling alleys, fast food outlets and multiplex cinemas.

The modern premises of the local *Sentinel* newspaper occupy the original site of Wedgwood's pottery before subsidence and pollution forced the company to move to Barlaston (Map 9). All that remains of the pottery is an enigmatic roundhouse, one of a pair which fronted the works.

ETRURIA JUNCTION has all the ingredients of a compelling canalscape and ought to claim a spot in most enthusiasts' "Alternative Seven Wonders of the Waterways" along with such acquired taste locations as Windmill End, Wigan Pier and Trent Falls. Much of Etruria's surviving charm emanates from the juxtaposition of the two top locks of the Stoke Five and the handsomely constructed and resonantly named Etruscan Bone Mill lying beside a small arm issuing from the tail of the second lock down. This now houses the Etruria Industrial Museum, the entrance to which is beside the Caldon Canal. Also of interest

is the old graving dock, an intriguing milepost to Uttoxeter, a statue of Brindley, and the proximity of the deep staircase locks at the start of the Caldon Canal, all good stuff for the diehard to get their teeth into. Etruria's busy basin lay on the outside of the sharp bend at the commencement of the Caldon Canal. It did not always deal solely in goods. In the 1840s, during a time of recession for the pottery trade, large numbers of emigrants began a long, life-changing journey

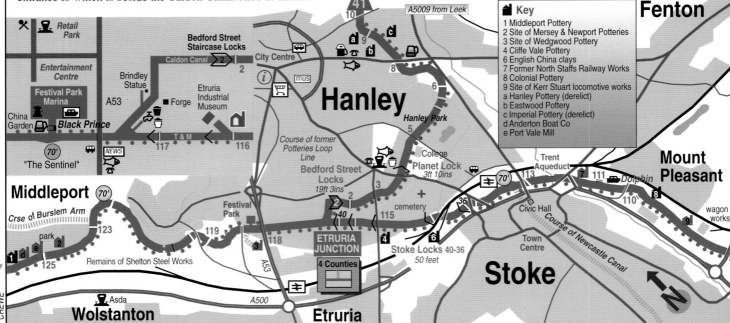

Key
1 Middleport Pottery
2 Site of Mersey & Newport Potteries
3 Site of Wedgwood Pottery
4 Cliffe Vale Pottery
6 English China clays
7 Former North Staffs Railway Works
8 Colonial Pottery
9 Site of Kerr Stuart locomotive works
a Hanley Pottery (derelict)
b Eastwood Pottery
c Imperial Pottery (derelict)
d Anderton Boat Co
e Port Vale Mill

*Figures refer to Trent & Mersey, allow 1 hour for Caldon Canal

aboard narrowboats from this wharf, destined for Wisconsin in North America, where a township named Pottersville was established.

Southwards from Etruria, the Trent & Mersey negotiates STOKE LOCKS, a fascinating flight, brim-full of images jostling for your attention: a ruined flour mill by the third lock down; a cemetery providing a splash of green in a sea of otherwise grey industry; a railway bridge carrying a siding into English China Clays' works (which receives this commodity in rail tankers now, whereas once it would have been brought round the coast from Cornwall to the Mersey and transhipped into narrowboats for the journey down to The Potteries) and the bottom lock in the flight, deep and concrete lined, a rebuilding dating from construction of the adjacent Queensway.

By Bridge 113, the NEWCASTLE-UNDER-LYME Canal once diverged from the main line. Opened in 1798, it ran in a V shape for 4 miles to the nearby borough of that name which, curiously, already had a canal. The Sir Nigel Gresley Canal, a three mile private waterway unconnected with any other canals, had opened in 1775 to carry coal from outlying collieries belonging to the Gresley family into Newcastle itself. The Newcastle Junction Canal was subsequently built to link the two canals, but an inclined plane, planned to bridge the disparity in height between the two 'Newcastle' canals, was never constructed. Not surprisingly, all three canals were early casualties of the Railway Age. Stoke Boat Club used the first few hundred yards of the canal as moorings in the Sixties, but all trace of the entrance vanished with construction of the adjacent dual carriageway.

Road and railway escort the canal out of Stoke like two hefty nightclub bouncers ejecting a customer who has failed the sartorial test. But the Trent & Mersey preserves its dignity, crossing the tiny Trent, passing a boatyard, and heading out into open county beneath the new A50 link road and past the city's refuse incinerator. Our map shows the site of Kerr Stuart's locomotive works where L.T.C. Rolt served an apprenticeship for three years from 1928. He writes as vividly as always about his days in Stoke in *Landscape With Machines*, his first volume of autobiography.

On the opposite bank of the canal, across the A500, is the site of Stoke City's former Victoria Ground, demolished when the club moved to their new Britannia Stadium just along the cut (see Map 9).

The Caldon Canal

Inland navigators, setting off from Etruria on the thirty mile trip to Uttoxeter, inferred by the milepost at the junction, are in for a disappointment. They can travel for seventeen miles to the remote wharf at Froghall, hidden deep in the woodlands of the Churnet Valley, but the canal onwards from that point to Uttoxeter itself was filled in and converted into a railway a century and a half ago. Nevertheless, the Caldon is one of the most delightful waterways in England, a thing of rare beauty, all the more enchanting because it is unfathomably under-utilised; though perhaps this only adds to its appeal in the eyes of connoisseurs.

From Etruria the Caldon Canal immediately declares its intentions, ascending a deep pair of staircase locks, followed by another single lock as it skirts Hanley, chief of the Six Towns. Dipping through an overbridge, it runs beside a stone wall over which peeps a typical Northern terrace. This simple throwback explains eloquently enough the inherent pathos of The Potteries: backyards with rainwater tubs and washing-lines; cobbled alleyways patrolled by stray dogs; net curtains blown softly by draughts unhampered by double-glazing. In another place, not far to the North, you would immediately think of Lowry or Coronation Street. But these are The Potteries, as warming, full of flavour, and insusceptible to the march of time as a Wrights steak & kidney pie.

Beyond Planet Lock the canal bisects HANLEY PARK, passing beneath a series of ornamental bridges. From a balcony embellished with terracotta, steps climb to a clock-towered pavilion from which you half expect Arnold Bennett characters to emerge at any moment.

Then follows a sad corridor of pottery works, for the most part derelict now, yet only a few years ago they were served by specially built craft carrying crockery from one department to another. This trade amounted to the final commercial use of a narrow canal anywhere in Britain. When we first covered this route in the mid 1980s the crockery boats worked out as far as Milton. Time was money and they didn't hang about. When you encountered one it was invariably accompanied by a tidal wave. As for the pottery factories, it is difficult to see any future other than demolition. And what then? More retail parks we'll be bound!

Continued on Map 41, page 69

Hanley (Map 8)

Arnold Bennett, his tongue perhaps not entirely in his cheek, called his 'Hanbridge' the Chicago of the Five Towns, which was his way of clarifying the confusing situation whereby it is Hanley that is the commercial heart of Stoke-on-Trent. Stoke is just one of the six communities, along with Tunstall, Burslem, Hanley itself, Longton and Fenton, that were merged to form Britain's fourteenth largest city in 1910. In any case the people of The Potteries have never been enamoured with the concept of belonging to an amorphous whole, preferring to shelter within the proudly individual characters of the six constituent towns. Hanley has suffered most from the pressures of the Consumer Age, and development has exorcised a good deal of the previously entrenched atmosphere of dignified northern provincialism. Heavens above, there is even a 'cultural quarter' now, something that would have Bennett choking on his Parisian cocktail had it occurred within his lifetime.

Cultural Quarter or not, one senses that 'eating-out' is still not an activity buried deep in The Potteries psyche, consequently there is a dearth of the sort of restaurants and cafe bars you would expect a twenty-first century city centre to provide. Most of the bars and pubs continue to pay lip service to the past, shyly offering 'tea with bread & butter' for their reactionary clientel. Undaunted we sent our 'glamour girls' into town with instructions to find a sophisticated establishment or perish in the attempt. They came up with LA-BODEGA, a Spanish tapas bar on Piccadilly (Tel: 01782 273322) offering "tasty Tapas dishes and accompanamientos, an excellent choice of Rioja wines, San Miguel, and a great salsa atmosphere!"
CHINA GARDEN (Tel: 01782 260199), beside the Festival Park Marina and built specifically for the National Garden Festival, offers 'family fare' at reasonable prices.
There are a number of fast food outlets within the precincts of the Festival Park in easy reach of the canal. There is also a HARVESTER restaurant adjacent to the Britannia Stadium on the southern outskirts of Stoke - see Map 9, though with the incinerator nearby mooring is not exactly salubrious.

All facilities are available in the centre of Hanley which is about 20 minutes walk from the Trent & Mersey Canal at Etruria, but less distant from the Caldon Canal at Bridges 4 or 8. Frequent buses run from stops on Bridge 118. THE POTTERIES CENTRE houses all the usual chain stores, whilst the MARKET HALL also provides an outlet for local retailing. North Staffordshire delicacies include 'oatcakes' and 'pikelets'; whilst Wrights have a number of shops and stalls selling their popular meat pies. Hanley is also well endowed with bookshops, both new and antiquarian, most of which stock an interesting selection of local titles. Numerous pottery works throughout the area have their own factory shops and visitor centres - a leaflet detailing these may be obtained from the Tourist Information Centre - see below. Closer to the canal, there is a retail area at Festival Park dominated by a huge Morrisons supermarket.
TOURIST INFORMATION CENTRE - Quadrant Road, Hanley ST1 1RZ. Tel: 01782 236000.
POTTERIES MUSEUM & ART GALLERY - Bethesda Street, Hanley. Tel: 01782 232323. Open daily (afternoon only on Sunday), admission free. A superb museum which puts those of many larger cities to shame. The world's finest collection of Staffordshire ceramics, a section devoted to local man Reginald Mitchell's Spitfire fighter plane, and a rich collection of drawings, paintings and prints.
ETRURIA INDUSTRIAL MUSEUM - canalside Bridge 116 (entrance beside the Caldon Canal). Open Wed-Sun 10am-4pm. Admission charge. Tel: 01782 287557. Cafe and small shop. Restored potters mill of exceptional interest. The mill dates from 1857 and was built to grind animal bones for use in 'bone' china. Beam engine steamed monthly. Adjacent blacksmith forge open to the public Wed-Sun 10am-4pm.
FESTIVAL PARK - Etruria. Access from canal via Bridge 118. Attractions include: multi-screen cinema (Tel: 01782 215311); Waterworld swimming centre (283838); dry ski slope (204159); bowling alley etc.
BUSES - Excellent services throughout The Potteries. Tel: 01782 207999. Vehicles display such evocative destination blinds as "Brown Edge", "Ubberley", "Fegg Hayes" and "Talke Pits".

Stoke (Map 8)

Known as 'Knype' in Arnold Bennett's stories, Stoke was, and still is, the railhead for The Potteries. Here, his Five Towns characters waited for the old Loop Line trains to take them to 'Hanbridge' (Hanley), 'Bleakridge' (Cobridge) and 'Bursley' (Burslem). The station itself is an architectural gem, a sort of Jacobean mansion with platforms where you would expect to find the croquet lawn. Across Winton Square, with its statue of Josiah Wedgwood, stands an equally imposing hotel. In the town itself the town hall and parish church make enduring architectural statements, but elsewhere the effect is largely lacklustre, and interest in the town is reliant on the proliferation of pottery works and factory shops.
TRAINS - major railhead adjacent to Bridge 113. Tel: 0845 484950. Useful connections with Stone and Kidsgrove for towpath walks.

Barlaston (Map 9)

Suburbia has engulfed Barlaston, but uphill, over the level crossing, a by-road winds attractively through older parts of the village and Wedgwood's pottery works, making for a pleasant short circular walk when combined with the towpath between bridges 103 and 104. There's a useful row of shops west of Bridge 103 including chemist, Spar, butcher, greengrocer and newsagent.
WEDGWOOD - adjacent Bridge 104. Visitor centre open daily throughout the year. Tel: 01782 204218 "Living museum, art gallery, gift shop, cinema, displays by skilled craftsmen."

Hem Heath (Map 9)

Popular suburban stopping point with boaters. Handy shop and TOBY INNS steak bar - Tel: 01782 657316.

Bottle kiln survivors at Etruria

Negotiating anglers - southbound out of Stoke

EVERY city has its soft underbellys of suburbia, and Hem Heath is one of Stoke's; more so now that its colliery has been closed and razed to the ground. Following privatisation, there was a brave attempt to reopen the mine, though sadly this just postponed the inevitable. It's cheaper, it would appear, to buy coal from Australia nowadays than dig for it locally.

Blue brick abutments mark the course of the Trentham branch railway which, in its brief heyday, carried hordes of North Staffordshire day-trippers to the gardens of Trentham Hall. Trentham had been the seat of the Dukes of Sutherland, the most recent property having been completed in 1842 to the designs of Sir Charles Barry, architect of the Houses of Parliament. By all accounts it had been a most beautiful house set in the loveliest of landscaped parklands and Italian gardens. However, the Trent ran through these gorgeous grounds and, as the river grew more and more polluted by the combined effluents of The Potteries, life for the Duke, his household and visitors - which often included royalty - became less and less idyllic. Eventually the Duke was forced to quit Trentham for another of the family seats, and the hall was demolished just before the Great War. He left the grounds to the people of The Potteries and, as more sophisticated methods of sewage control were developed, Trentham Gardens became a celebrated resort for the residents of North Staffordshire. A tall monument commemorating the second Duke of Sutherland may be seen rising above woodlands to the west of Trentham Lock.

TRENTHAM LOCK boasts a deep chamber with a pronounced undertow when filling. The foundations of its erstwhile keeper's cottage are readily apparent. Nearby stands the famous pottery works of Wedgwood. The company moved to Barlaston from their original site at Etruria in 1940. The new plant departed from the traditional design of pottery works in many ways, not least the adoption of electric tunnel ovens in place of bottle kilns.

The great Palladian facade of Barlaston Hall gazes benignly over the canal between bridges 103 and 104. Once there were fears that subsidence caused by mining at the former Hem Heath colliery, which finally closed in the mid Nineties, might bring about its demolition, but now it is in the process of being refurbished by English Heritage. Next door stands a church abandoned because of the same threat of subsidence. A new church, paid for by British Coal, has been erected in Barlaston village.

Barlaston is a popular overnight mooring point - details of its amenities, and of the Wedgwood Pottery Visitor Centre, appear on Page 20. At one time there was a busy boatbuilding yard here. A row of cottages occupied by its workforce - now highly desirable properties indeed - may be observed on the offside south of Bridge 103.

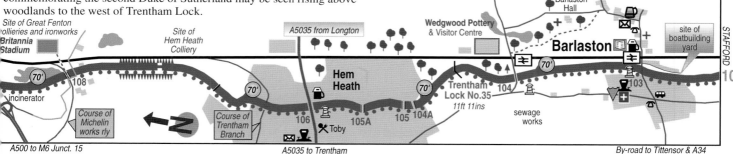

MAKING its way through the upper valley of the Trent, the canal encounters the market town of Stone, original headquarters of the Trent & Mersey Canal Company. It lost its role as the administrative centre for the canal when it was bought out by the North Staffordshire Railway in 1846, but retained an extensive dockyard for maintenance purposes, whilst many of the town's once interesting array of industries used the canal for transport. Nowadays the emphasis is obviously on leisure use, and there is still much to see as you chug through the four locks of the Stone flight.

The top lock, known as Limekiln, is situated on the northern edge of town, near the railway station with its distinctive 'Dutch' gabled booking-hall. The next lock down is Newcastle Road, overlooked by a large convent school; a boat horse tunnel leads underneath the road to a busy pound occupied by two hire fleets and with extensive linear moorings for private boats. The former ale stores of Joule's Brewery overlook the canal before it widens by a fascinating spread of docks, covered and uncovered, wet and dry. These belong to the Canal Cruising Company, a pioneer of boating holidays on the canals, having been founded in 1948. It was here that L.T.C. Rolt's boat *Cressy* of *Narrow Boat* fame met its end, being broken up and cremated after failing a survey in 1951.

Yard Lock, located beside the boatyard, is the deepest of the flight. On the other side of the canal the town's former hospital - once a workhouse - stands derelict, a sorry sight indeed, especially for those waiting two years for a hip operation. The gas works stood beside the next pound on a site now given over to car parking.

Star Lock is the bottom chamber in the flight. The pub from which it derived the name dates from the 16th century. An old warehouse on the offside below Bridge 93 has been converted into retirement flats, whilst several new buildings have been erected beside it in a pleasingly harmonious style. The canal company's offices stood alongside the towpath at this point, though there is no evidence of these now. They were demolished after the war, having been used for many years as a chocolate factory. Arguably the best moorings for access to the town are provided here, alongside a sportsground and children's play area.

There are also four locks in the MEAFORD flight; the locals say "Method". Originally three of them were combined as a 'staircase'. Traces of the old course of the canal can clearly be seen to the west of the present layout. Meaford Locks form an attractive group and are bordered by a country road with stone walling; one of the first signs that the Midlands are beginning to give way to the North.

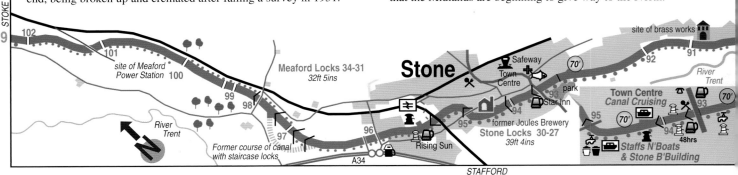

Stone

Stone is a bustling little market town with a rich and varied history. Conscious of their heritage, the local civic society have erected plaques on walls recalling that Peter de Wint, the landscape watercolourist, was born here; that the Duke of Cumberland came here to do battle; that the "Star Inn" has long attended to the thirst of passers-by; and that in roughly a hundred years from now a leading member of the community will be entitled to open a memory vault secreted in a cask beneath the old entrance arch of Joules Brewery. The demise of Joules remains Stone's great sadness. This proud independent had been brewing in the town since 1758 and, with the advent of the canal and the possibilities of export it brought, their ales became fashionable in Europe and the Americas. Once they operated a pair of boats to bring in coal for firing the steam plant. As late as the fifties their office retained the telephone number 'Stone 1'. But in 1970 they were taken over by the Bass Charrington conglomerate and, not unexpectedly, brewing ceased four years later though the canalside ale stores remain intact. Bents, the town's other brewers, closed in the early 1960s.

STAR INN - canalside Bridge 93. Quaint Banks's lockside pub serving bar meals. Tel: 01785 813096.

SWAN INN - Lichfield Street (adjacent Bridge 93). Lively town centre local.

RISING SUN - adjacent Limekiln Lock. Families are welcome at this comfortable Bass pub. Bar lunches and dinners daily except Sundays. Canalside garden with swings etc. Tel: 01785 813494.

LA DOLCE VITA - canalside Star Lock. Really nice lock-side Italian. Tel: 01785 817985.

HATTERS - Newcastle Road (adjacent Bridge 95). Well regarded restaurant with a varied menu. Tel: 01785 819292.

CASA LOCO - Radford Street (access via Bridge 93). Mexican restaurant with atmosphere, Tequila, La Bamba, the lot. Tel: 01785 813137.

AL SHEIKH'S - Lichfield Street. Good Balti. Tel: 01785 819684.

Stone is a good shopping centre with the advantage of being so close to the canal that you can easily carry heavy carrier-bags back to the boat. Nice cakes from Hammersleys bakery on High Street. Somerfield and Safeway supermarkets. Market on Tuesdays, Fridays & Saturdays. Antiques from The Gallery by Bridge 93.

BUSES - Services to/from Stafford and Hanley. Tel: 01782 207999.
TRAINS - local trains to/from Stoke and Stafford. Tel: 08457 484950.

Meaford Locks, Trent & Mersey Canal near Stone

TAKING apparent pleasure in each other's company, canal and river, road and railway make their undemonstrative way through a shallow valley, skirting, but scarcely encountering, a succession of small settlements, barely in the category of villages. With no great dramas to catch the eye, the canal traveller is thrown back on his own resources. He can pass the time wrestling with the great conundrums of life or anticipate the slow drawing of a pint in the cool bars of the "Greyhound" at Burston or the "Dog & Doublet" at Sandon.

ASTON LOCK marks the half-way point of the Trent & Mersey's route from Preston Brook to Shardlow; names which mean nothing now but were once as well known as Spaghetti Junction and Watford Gap. One of the distinctive cast iron mileposts, originally made in Stone by Rangeley & Dixon, quotes 46 miles in either direction. Those that have been lost down the years have been replaced with replicas by the Trent & Mersey Canal Society; a laudable and imaginative contribution to conservation.

It is but a short stroll from SANDON LOCK to the picturesque village of the same name. Sandon Hall, home of the Harrowbys, is a Victorian house in Jacobean style, well hidden from the world in rolling parkland. Above the woods peeps a slender urn-topped column commemorating William Pitt. Another Prime Minister, the assassinated Spencer Perceval, is remembered in a nearby shrine. Unfortunately the house and its grounds are only occasionally open to the public, but you can walk up the hill with the pheasants to the isolated church of All Saints to gain a panoramic view of the Trent Valley. Other points of interest in Sandon include the war memorial at the crossroads, the quaint 'arts & crafts' style village hall and matching pub, and the ornate former station house, notable for the *porte-cochere*, built to accommodate the carriage from Sandon Hall.

If you are undertaking a full circuit of the FOUR COUNTIES RING it is rewarding to contrast the character of the Trent & Mersey Canal with the Shropshire Union; barely ten miles away across country but a world away in style and atmosphere. Here the canal winds apparently arbitarily beneath mellow brick accommodation bridges in a Georgian apothesis of grace, whilst the 'Shroppie', with its sturdy stone bridges, bold straights and Victorian sense of purpose, exudes an altogether different ambience.

Summary of Facilities

There are congenial country inns at Burston and Sandon: THE GREYHOUND (Tel: 01889 508263) and DOG & DOUBLET (Tel: 01889 508331) respectively. Both serve meals lunchtimes and evenings, the latter being open all day and offering both accommodation and a skittle alley. Sandon also has a useful roadside stores and a post office.

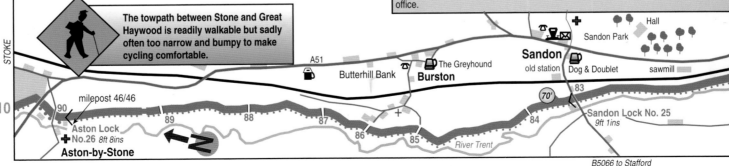

The towpath between Stone and Great Haywood is readily walkable but sadly often too narrow and bumpy to make cycling comfortable.

STOKE

A51

Butterhill Bank

The Greyhound

Burston

Sandon

old station   Dog & Doublet   sawmill

Hall

Sandon Park

milepost 46/46

90

89   88   87   86   85   *River Trent*

84   83

70'

Aston Lock
No.26 8ft 8ins

Aston-by-Stone

10

Sandon Lock No. 25
9ft 1ins

B5066 to Stafford

Busy day at Sandon Lock

27

WANDERING through a gracious landscape, planned and planted for posterity by the gentry of Sandon, Weston and Ingestre, the Trent & Mersey Canal continues its relationship with the Trent Valley, basking in rural tranquillity, a linear hymn of resilient charm. Given the beauty of the countryside, it is no coincidence that several wealthy and influential families put down grandiose roots here. How did they perceive the arrival of Brindley's canal? Were they excited by its potential or fearful of its intrusion? History records that almost without exception the gentlemen of Staffordshire were in favour of the canal. Perhaps they saw only the financial advantages which might accrue from its construction, and not that it could be a precursor of change in their hitherto orderly and immutable world. Built of brick and stone for the benefit of Sandon's gentry, Bridge 82 echoes the high aesthetic values of the 18th century.

Any scar tissue wrought by the advent of the canal must have been healed by the time the railways arrived. The North Staffordshire Railway followed the course of the Trent & Mersey (which it was soon to acquire) down the valley to Colwich and became a main line of some importance as a through route

between Manchester and London via The Potteries. Another line arrived in the landscape, was absorbed into the Great Northern Railway and became a far flung outpost of the LNER at the grouping of the railway companies in 1923. Passenger traffic was never significant - how could it be in these rural haunts? - but the milk of the Trent Valley's cows was creamy enough for the scheduling of a daily milk train to the capital.

One activity in this otherwise rural area that the canal did help to prosper was the making of salt. The Trentside village of that name has associations with the trade going back to Medieval times; perhaps even Roman. But at both Shirleywich and Weston brine pumping developed significantly because the canal was used to bring in coal to fuel evaporation and to carry the finished product to market.

Weston-on-Trent

You can sit on the village green outside the highly recommended WOOLPACK (Tel: 01889 270238) after a hard day's boating, sample the SARACEN'S HEAD (Tel: 01889 270286) or stroll uphill to the restaurant facilties in WESTON HALL (Tel: 01889 271700) which opens for morning coffee at 10am, lunch at noon (not Mons) and for dinner at 6.30pm (not Mons or Suns).

With bicylces on board it's an easy detour to AMERTON WORKING FARM (Tel: 01889 271300) an entertaining mix of craft shops and farm animals with a narrow gauge railway to boot. Regular buses to Stafford and Uttoxeter (Tel: 01785 223344). The village store is open daily.

A518 from Uttoxeter
Amerton Working Farm 1 mile

Weston-on-Trent

Pitt's Column

Gayton Brook

80

81

Woolpack

timber yard

M. Braine

Saracen's Head

Course of former Great Northern Rly.

Weston Wharf

Weston Lock No.24 8ft 0ins

79

River Trent

Shirleywich
site of salt works

70'

78

A51

Pasturefields

77

76

Hoo Mill Lock No.23 7ft 9ins
E & C Services

11

82

Salt

Weston Hall

A518 to Stafford

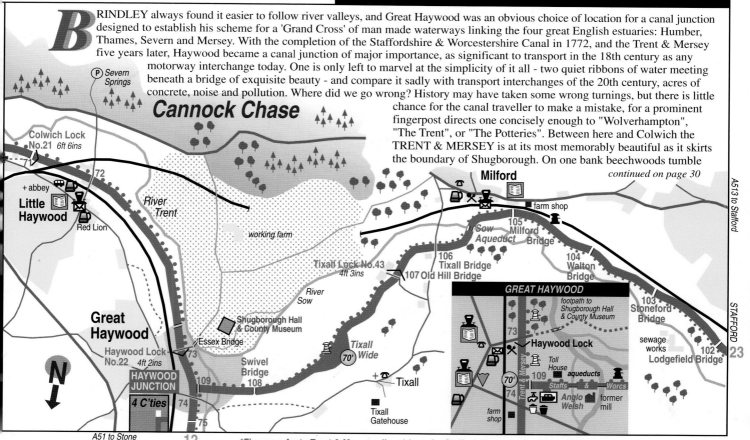

BRINDLEY always found it easier to follow river valleys, and Great Haywood was an obvious choice of location for a canal junction designed to establish his scheme for a 'Grand Cross' of man made waterways linking the four great English estuaries: Humber, Thames, Severn and Mersey. With the completion of the Staffordshire & Worcestershire Canal in 1772, and the Trent & Mersey five years later, Haywood became a canal junction of major importance, as significant to transport in the 18th century as any motorway interchange today. One is only left to marvel at the simplicity of it all - two quiet ribbons of water meeting beneath a bridge of exquisite beauty - and compare it sadly with transport interchanges of the 20th century, acres of concrete, noise and pollution. Where did we go wrong? History may have taken some wrong turnings, but there is little chance for the canal traveller to make a mistake, for a prominent fingerpost directs one concisely enough to "Wolverhampton", "The Trent", or "The Potteries". Between here and Colwich the TRENT & MERSEY is at its most memorably beautiful as it skirts the boundary of Shugborough. On one bank beechwoods tumble

continued on page 30

Map labels:

P Severn Springs

Colwich Lock No.21 6ft 6ins

Cannock Chase

+ abbey

Little Haywood

Red Lion

River Trent

working farm

Great Haywood

Shugborough Hall & County Museum

Essex Bridge

Haywood Lock No.22 4ft 2ins

Swivel Bridge 108

HAYWOOD JUNCTION

4 C'ties

N

A51 to Stone

Tixall Lock No.43 4ft 3ins

River Sow

Tixall Wide 70'

Tixall

Tixall Gatehouse

Milford

Sow Aqueduct

105 Milford Bridge

106

107 Old Hill Bridge

Tixall Bridge

104 Walton Bridge

103 Stoneford Bridge

sewage works

102 Lodgefield Bridge

farm shop

A513 to Stafford

STAFFORD

23

GREAT HAYWOOD

footpath to Shugborough Hall & County Museum

73

Haywood Lock

Toll House

Staffs & Worcs aqueducts

109

74

Anglo Welsh

former mill

farm shop

Trent & Mersey

70'

12

Figures refer to Trent & Mersey, allow 1 hour for Staffs & Worcs bridge 109 to 102

continued from page 29

down to the water's edge. On the other, across the Trent, lies the folly-peppered grounds of the Anson family's famous home. Colwich Lock lies in an attractive setting between the village church, a picturesquely decrepit farm and a bend in the river. From Bridge 72 you can take an idyllic walk to Severn Springs and on up into The Chase itself.

The Staffordshire & Worcestershire Canal

Through the arch of Bridge 109 - an 18th century fusion of functional engineering and enduring loveliness - the Staffordshire & Worcestershire Canal can be seen heading westwards on its 46 mile journey down to the Severn at Stourport. Two aqueducts carry it across the Trent and a millstream. A couple of miles further on it crosses the Sow. Between these river crossings the canal suddenly casts off its inhibitions and widens into a broad lake, bordered by thick reedbeds inhabited by a gorgeous array of wildfowl. This is Tixall Wide or Broadwater and there are two theories for its existence. Some maintain that the canal was widened into an artificial lake to placate the owner of Tixall Hall. Others that the expanse of water predates the canal, that it was naturally formed, and that Izaak Walton learnt to fish here. Whichever explanation suits you, don't miss the extraordinary Elizabethan gatehouse which overlooks the Wide. It is available for let by the Landmark Trust - Tel: 01628 825925. The hall itself, where Mary Queen of Scots was imprisoned for a fortnight in 1586, was demolished long ago. West of Tixall's solitary lock the canal meanders enchantingly through the valley of the Sow. *Continued on Map 23*

The beautiful bridge at Haywood Junction

The Haywoods *(Map 13)*

The villages of Great and Little Haywood are separated by the long, high brick wall of the Shugborough estate. Dormitory housing has inevitably expanded both populations, but the centres remain peaceful and largely unspoilt; especially so in the charming lane leading from Great Haywood, under the railway and over the canal to the Essex Bridge, one of the finest examples of a packhorse bridge imaginable. On hot summer days the locals splash about in the water here as their forebears must have done for generations.

LOCK HOUSE RESTAURANT - adjacent Haywood Lock. Tel: 01889 881294. Morning coffee, afternoon teas, a la carte dinners. Also two pubs in each village.

Little Haywood has a post office stores and newsagent. Great Haywood has two general stores (one with a butcher's counter), a post office, and a farm shop alongside the junction. At the junction the former toll house is an outlet for canalware and crafts.

SHUGBOROUGH HALL - access via Haywood Lock and Essex Bridge. Open daily April to September. Admission charge. Attractions include mansion, county museum, working farm, gardens, National Trust shop and cafeteria. Regular special events. Tel: 01889 881388.

BUSES - regular services to Stafford from Little Haywood. Tel: 01785 223344.

Milford *(Map 13)*

The motorists' gateway to The Chase and thus too busy to hold much appeal for canallers. but there are some useful facilities if you're not averse to mooring alongside the busy railway, not least a farm shop accessed from the beautiful Bridge 105.

THE river's slow influence pervades the canal, and the pair wander across the landscape like indolent lovers on a long afternoon, chaperoned at a discreet distance by the recumbent mass of The Chase. Several big houses were built by prosperous landowners in this enchanting countryside. The stuccoed facade of Bishton Hall overlooks the canal. Nowadays it is a prep school with an idyllic cricket ground shaded by ancient chestnut trees bordering the water. Another mansion, Wolseley Hall, stood opposite on the far bank of the river. It was demolished long ago, but the grounds have been restored as ornamental gardens. Wolseley Bridge has graced the Trent here since 1800. It was designed by John Rennie, best known in canal circles for his work on the Kennet & Avon.

The towpath plays host to a pair of walking routes: the Staffordshire Way (Rudyard to Kinver) and Millennium Way (Newport to Burton-on-Trent). RUGELEY usually gets a bad press from guidebooks, but we have always had a soft spot for this down to earth little town, once home to the notorious Victorian poisoner, William Palmer

and recently remembered as the scene, in 1839, of the canal murder of Christina Collins. In years gone by Rugeley was the site of a malodorous tannery (where there are flats now at Bridge 66) but it's the power station which dominates now, being opened here in the Sixties to take advantage of coal mined on the spot; though the colliery has closed and nowadays coal is brought in by train from far and wide - often having originated beyond these shores.

At Brindley Bank the canal suddenly stops running parallel with the Trent and turns sharply to cross it, as though Brindley had been screwing up his courage to bridge the river. A handsome pumping station overlooks this crossing of water over water, though the aqueduct itself is of little aesthetic appeal.

By Bridge 68 a short, reedy arm adjacent to the railway provides a useful turning point for lengthy craft. This may have been used as a transhipment basin in the fledgling days of the railway, perhaps for the conveyance of building materials.

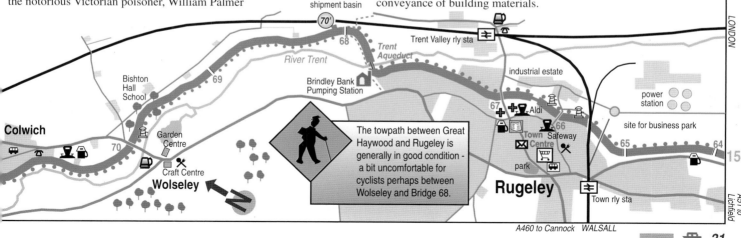

site of trans-shipment basin

70'

68

Trent Aqueduct

River Trent

Trent Valley rly sta

Bishton Hall School

69

Brindley Bank Pumping Station

industrial estate

power station

site for business park

Colwich

Garden Centre

70

Craft Centre

Wolseley

The towpath between Great Haywood and Rugeley is generally in good condition - a bit uncomfortable for cyclists perhaps between Wolseley and Bridge 68.

67

Aldi

66

Town Centre

Safeway

park

Rugeley

65

64

15

Town rly sta

LONDON

A51 to Lichfield

A460 to Cannock WALSALL

Brindley's aqueduct across the River Trent near Rugeley

Rugeley (Map 14)

A former mining town well versed in the vicissitudes of existence following the abandonment of the local pit in 1990. Scots accents are often to be heard, imigrants who came to work in the mine and remained washed-up by its cruel closure. It's difficult to escape the impression that life here is lived on the cheap, though not without a certain deadpan dignity. Here in the tight-knit streets, and on the old Coal Board estates, one finds thrift and graft and a perverse civic pride, whilst a consoling beauty is to be found up on the nearby Chase.

GEORGE & BERTIES - Albion Street. An unusual cafe with a central bar around which customers sit perched on high stools as if this were somewhere in Belgium. Tel: 01889 577071.

TERRAZZA - Italian restaurant housed in old chapel on Lichfield Street. Tel: 01889 570630.

RUGELEY KEBAB HOUSE - Anson Street. Fast food takeaway outlet - free local delivery. Tel: 01889 577677.

Despite appearances, shopping in Rugeley can be fun. Moor north of Bridge 66 for easiest access to nearby town centre. Safeway and Aldi supermarkets nearby. Market on Tue, Thur-Sat. Branches of the main banks.

BUSES - services throughout the Trent Valley and Cannock Chase. If you've time to spare take the Green Bus to Cannock, a magical mystery tour up and over The Chase. Tel: 01785 223344.

TRAINS - sparse weekday service along Trent Valley but more frequent from Town or Trent Valley stations to Stafford and Birmingham. Tel: 08457 484950.

Colwich & Wolseley (Map 14)

Two little communities strung out along the A51. Wolseley has a craft centre, antiques showroom, art gallery and garden centre all accessible from Bridge 70.

WOLSELEY ARMS - Tel: 01889 575133, once the meeting place for the promoters of the canal.

SHIMLA PALACE - Tel: 01889 881325. Indian restaurant, eat in or takeaway.

WHILST by no means a length of canal likely to endear itself to connoisseurs of the picturesque, this stretch of the Trent & Mersey is never actually overwhelmed by industry, and there are a number of invigorating views over the Trent Valley or up on to the flanks of Cannock Chase.

Armitage and Shanks are synonymous with toilet plumbing. Their trade marks are emblazoned on public conveniences throughout the world. Once they were separate firms, merging in 1969, but the site alongside the canal at ARMITAGE dates back to 1817. Sanitaryware became a speciality in the 19th century under the management of Edward Johns - the origin of the Americanism "Going to the John". Today the factory is huge and convincingly prosperous, and Armitage Shanks are a public limited company with a seemingly 'watertight' future. Connections are apparent with another famous earthenware firm at Spode House and Hawkesyard Priory. Josiah Spode, a member of the North Staffordshire pottery family, left his house to a Dominican Order in 1893 and the monks proceeded to build a priory in the gounds. The priory is now a nursing home whilst the house and its grounds have become a golf course.

Passing beneath the A513, the canal narrows and negotiates a rocky cutting. One-way working is the order of the day. This was formerly the site of Armitage (or "Plum Pudding") Tunnel, a dramatic unlined bore through the rock face. Subsidence, induced by coal mining, necessitated opening out of the tunnel, and concrete lining of the canal banks.

Handsacre

An unremarkable community, but the High Bridge spanning the Trent to the north of Bridge 58 is worth a look; its graceful single cast-iron arch made at Coalbrookdale in 1830. THE CROWN (Tel: 01543 490239) is a congenial Bass local where the repartee is apt to be as frothy as your pint. Frequent queues testify to the quality of the fish & chips from MICHAEL'S just up the road and there's a quaint cafe in the village too.

Armitage

Guidebooks point to the "interesting" church perched on a rocky bluff above the bosky canal by Bridge 61, but the village is dominated by the sanitaryware works. A path worth taking leads beneath the West Coast Main Line railway and over the Trent to the isolated settlement of Mavesyn Ridware.

There are a number of shops on the main road, though mooring can be problematical on what is a rather narrow and tortuous secton of canal.

Several eating out opportunities present themselves: SPODE COTTAGE a Tom Cobleigh family pub/restaurant (Tel: 01543 490353). THE PLUM PUDDING (Tel: 01543 490330), beside Bridge 61A, has dropped well below the level of the canal through subsidence, but retains its homely atmosphere - Ansell's and Marston's ales accompany a good choice of meals. Finally, there's the ASH TREE (Tel: 01889 578314), beside Bridge 62.

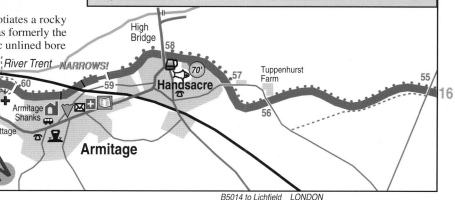

Abend in the canal south of Woodend Lock, and glimpses of the three spires of Lichfield Cathedral, tell you that you and the Trent & Mersey have travelled as far south as you are ever going to get in the canal's arc-like journey between Preston Brook and Shardlow. Ravenshaw Woods are a riot of rhododendron colour in early summer. The works by Bridge 54 was once the smelly "milk factory" referred to by L.T.C.Rolt in *Narrow Boat*.

FRADLEY JUNCTION'S fame far outweighs the sum of its parts. All that ever seems to change is the music emanating from the crowded interior of "The Swan". On hot summer days the junction is hugely popular with sightseers, but on winter afternoons it isn't difficult to imagine how it must have looked in the latter days of cargo carrying, as memorably described by Tom Foxon in his book of working boatman reminiscences, *Number One!*.

The Coventry Canal heads off in a southerly direction towards Fazeley and Tamworth - a route covered in our "South Midlands" and "Stourport Ring" Canal Companions. British Waterways' local manager and his staff occupy the neat former 'company' maintenance yard located between Keeper's and Junction locks. On the opposite bank private woodland masks Fradley Reservoir, built for the canal but nowadays rarely called upon to act as a feeder.

Between Fradley and Alrewas the canal crosses former common land and the flat nature of the adjoining fields engenders a distinct feeling of emptiness. The canal curves endearingly through the picturesque village of Alrewas, long ago a centre of basket weaving. Below Alrewas Lock the canal merges with the River Trent for a short distance before the river plunges unnervingly over a large weir. The towpath is carried over a mill stream, the main channel of the river, and a succession of reedy backwaters by an attractive series of metal footbridges.

Fradley Junction

The epitome of a rural canal junction, Fradley often attracts more motorists that it can comfortably deal with. The SWAN INN (Tel: 01283 790330) plays a key role in this popularity, coping manfully with customers whether they have come by water or road. Bar meals available and families are welcome.

See page 37 for details of Alrewas and its facilities.

Beware the current on the river section between Alrewas and Wychnor locks.

---

garden centre

15
A515 from Lichfield

54 Kings Bromley Wharf

Ravenshaw Wood

Woodend Lock No.20 *5ft 2ins*

53

FRADLEY JUNCTION
Junction Lock No.17 *8ft 0ins*
Swan Line
Middle Lock No.18 *7ft 6ins*
52
Shade (or Shed) House Lock No.19 *7ft 8ins*

Keeper's Lock No.16 *6ft 10ins*
50
51
British Waterways
91

Hunts Lock No.15 *5ft 8ins*

Common Lock No.14 *4ft 6ins*

49A
Bagnall Lock No.13 *5ft 7ins*
49

River Trent

A513 from Rugeley   mill

WEIR !

46   Alrewas Lock No.12 *5ft 8ins*
47
48

Alrewas

N

By-road to Lichfield

Coventry Canal ▼ to Fazeley

A38 to Birmingham   A513 to Tamworth

KEEPING company with the Roman's Ryknield Street, the canal traverses the broad, flat valley of the Trent; a landscape of gravel pits and distant villages backed by low-lying hills. Between Alrewas and WYCHNOR the canal suddenly assumes a quite different character as it negotiates a marshy, almost ethereal stretch of countryside, criss-crossed by drainage channels, or 'sitches', which thread their way through meadowlands to meet the Trent. It is a sudden, yet subtle, scene change. The domesticity of Alrewas village and the cacophony of the A38 are briefly forgotten, as the waterway puts you tantalisingly in touch with a past inhabited by eel-catchers, reed-cutters and sluice-keepers.

Wychnor was the scene of a tradition, similar to the more famous one at Dunmow in Essex, whereby any man who could swear not to have wished to exchange his wife for another woman, at any time during the first year of his marriage, was entitled to a flitch of bacon from the Lord of the Manor. It may - or may not - surprise you to learn that the flitch was never successfully claimed. Wychnor Church, reached from Bridge 45, dates back to the thirteenth century although the tower is a much later addition.

At BARTON TURNS wharves were provided for the villages of Barton and Walton, each a mile or so from the canal on opposite sides of the Trent. Good moorings are available here along with water and rubbish disposal facilities in a charming setting overlooked by an imposing Georgian wharf house. Fifteen minutes walk away, Barton-under-Needwood itself is a useful source of supplies and refreshment. When the bridge across the river to Walton was damaged by floods in the 1940s, it was replaced by a 'temporary' Bailey bridge - it's still in use! A large new marina offers moorings to the north of Barton Turns. There are ambitious plans to develop this for multi-recreational use.

TATENHILL LOCK lies in a deceptively remote setting. The former lock-keeper's house is now a private dwelling. A path runs from Bridge 35 between old gravel workings, and through a fragrant pig farm, in the direction of the village of Tatenhill, tucked demurely away between folds of the Needwood Hills. The Forest of Needwood was once one of the largest Royal hunting grounds; little woodland now remains, although trees are returning with the establishment of the new National Forest.

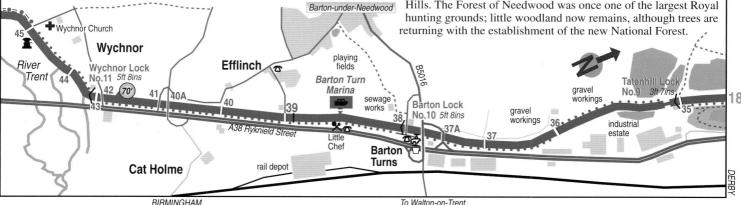

THE brewery town of Burton-on-Trent presides over the Trent & Mersey Canal's change of gauge: east of Dallow Lane the locks will be widebeam. When the canal opened in 1770, it brought a rapid decline in the use of the River Trent, which had itself been made navigable up to Burton at the beginning of the 18th century. To serve wharves established on the riverbank, however, a branch canal was built from Shobnall to Bond End. When the Birmingham & Derby Junction Railway was opened a drawbridge was provided to carry the line over this Bond End Canal. In 1846 a southbound train plunged into the canal because the bridge had been opened for the passage of a boat in the mistaken belief that no train was due!

Bridge 34 at BRANSTON is a popular mooring point for boaters attracted by the canalside pub. Beyond the towpath hedge the adjoining flooded-out gravel workings have been transformed into a 'water park'. Between Branston and Shobnall the canals runs at the foot of an escarpment marking the edge of what was once the forest of Needwood. The half-timbered house on the hill is Sinai Park which belonged to the Benedictine monastery founded in the town in 1004. The main part of the abbey lay beside the river, but Sinai Park was used variously as a hunting lodge, summer house and blood-letting sanatorium.

It is at SHOBNALL that the canal traveller becomes most aware of Burton-on-Trent's stock in trade. West of the canal stands Marston's brewery, to the east the Bass maltings. Visitors are quick to remark upon the aroma of hops in the vicinity, though locals are largely inured to the aromatic tang of the town. A common misapprehension is that Burton derives its excellence in brewing from Trent water. In fact the water used for brewing lies on beds of gypsum rock beneath the town and is pumped to the surface. The predominance of such stone made Burton a centre for the production of alabaster ornaments in the middle ages.

One of the once numerous branch railways, linking the main lines with Burton's breweries and other industries, paralleled the canal on its way through the town. Nowadays it's used as a public footpath and cycleway. In its heyday, Burton's 'internal' railway system was so dense that there were 32 level crossings in the town. The railways captured the bulk of beer transport from the canal, but at the end of the 18th century large volumes of ale were being exported via Hull to northern Europe, the Baltic and Russia, and via Liverpool to India and South America.

Until the late 1970s the basin at HORNINGLOW was overlooked by a salt warehouse, part of which actually spanned the canal, so that boats heading east appeared to vanish into a 'tunnel'.

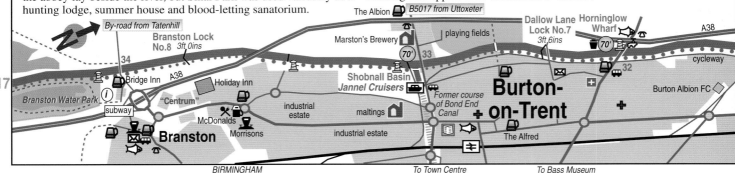

The Albion · B5017 *from Uttoxeter*

By-road from Tatenhill

Branston Lock No.8 *3ft 0ins*

Marston's Brewery

playing fields

Dallow Lane Horninglow Lock No.7 Wharf *3ft 6ins*

A38

34

Bridge Inn · A38

Holiday Inn

70'

33

70'

32

cycleway

17

Branston Water Park

i

subway

"Centrum"

Shobnall Basin *Jannel Cruisers*

Former course of Bond End Canal

Burton-on-Trent

Burton Albion FC

McDonalds

Morrisons

industrial estate

maltings

industrial estate

The Alfred

Branston

BIRMINGHAM · To Town Centre · To Bass Museum

Alrewas (Map 16)

A fundamentally pretty village not entirely compromised by the grafting on of new housing. Sadly the animal feeds mill has ceased to function commercially, though one envies its new domestic occupants. Pronounced 'Ol-re-wuss', the name is derived from the presence of alder trees in the vicinity which were used in basket making. The 14th century church close to Bridge 47 is worth a visit. - and, yes, there's *still* a donkey grazing contentedly in the adjoining thistly field.

THE CROWN - Post Office Road. Tel: 01283 790328. Lively local.
GEORGE & DRAGON - Main Street. Tel: 01283 791476. Marston's pub offering a wide choice of bar meals.
RAFTERS RESTAURANT - Main Street. Tel: 01283 790202. Popular restaurant adjacent to "George & Dragon".
THE OLD BOAT- beside Bagnall Lock. Tel: 01283 791468. Plus fish & chips and a Chinese takeaway.

The village has a couple of admirable shops. BARKERS (up along the main street towards the A38) dates back to 1924 and has an unexpectedly ambitious selecton of wines and fine foods, whilst COATES the butcher has a wide choice of game. Also: an off licence, chemist, newsagent and Co-op store open late Mon-Sat.

BUSES - Regular services to/from Burton and Lichfield. Tel: 01785 223344.

Barton-under-Neewood (Map 17)

Mellifluously named but much enlarged village with good shopping facilities and several pubs approachable via footpath or B5016. Bar meals available at the BARTON TURNS (Tel: 01283 712142), canalside by Bridge 38.

Branston (Map 18)

Once a village, and ostensibly (though probably not) the birthplace of the eponymous pickle relish, now a fast expanding suburb useful for its facilities.
BRIDGE INN - canalside Bridge 34. Tel: 01283 564177. Characterful former boatman's pub where draught "Pedigree" is still served straight from the barrel. Good choice of meals and a pleasant canalside garden.
Through the underpass, Branston also boasts a fish & chip shop, a Chinese take-away and two other pubs.
Use the subway beneath the road interchange to reach the shops, five minutes walk from Bridge 34. Facilities include: 'early-late' store, post office, and butcher.

Burton-on-Trent (Map 18)

It is difficult to write dispassionately about one's home town. Affection collides with contempt; and there are casualties. But with a courteous nod in the mellower directions of Tadcaster, Hook Norton and Southwold, this is the definitive brewery town, albeit one rendered increasingly anodyne as merger suceeds merger. At the turn of the century there were over twenty breweries in the town, but rationalisation has reduced this to just two large concerns, Bass and Marstons, plus a small independent, the Burton Bridge Brewery. So "Beertown-on-Trent" still reverberates to its stock in trade, though for anyone who knew it prior to the contraction of the brewing industry and the closure of its quaint network of interconnecting railway lines, the place is an 'Indian Pale' shadow of its former self. A regretable casualty of Progress has been the bulk of Burton's brewing infrastructure. Compare the realistic model in the Bass Museum with the present's dour reality, and you too will mourn the loss of so many maltings and brewing plants. Nowadays the most pleasant aspects of the town are to be had from the riverside. Perhaps it was always so, for this was where the monks chose to erect their long vanished abbey.

THE ALBION - third of a mile to north of Shobnall Basin. A Marston's pub with a large garden and a good range of meals. Tel: 01283 568197.
BILL BREWER - Centrum, Branston. Tom Cobleigh family pub. Tel: 01283 517231.
THE MILL HOUSE - canalside Bridge 29A, Map 19. All day family pub. Tel: 01283 535133.
BURTON BRIDGE - mile south of Horninglow Wharf. Worth the long trek to sample the town's micro-brewery. Unspoilt atmosphere, lunchtime snacks. Tel: 01283 536596.

THE ALFRED - Derby Street. Burton Bridge's second pub. Excellent bar meals. Tel: 01283 562178.
COOPERS TAVERN - Cross Street (2nd right beyond railway station). Famously basic ale house - now serves Kimberley.Tel: 01283 532551.

The town centre is 15-20 dispiriting minutes walk from the canal, though buses operate from both Horninglow and Shobnall basins. Closer at hand there are shops along the length of Waterloo Street easily reached from Dallow Lane and Shobnall. Market days Thur-Sat. MORRISONS supermarket is nearest the canal (along with McDONALDS) at Branston.

(i) BASS MUSEUM - Horninglow Street (10 mins walk from Horninglow Wharf) Tel: 01283 542031. Open daily, admission charge. Fascinating displays of the development of Burton brewing. Shire horse and rail and road transport exhibits. Mock-up of Horninglow Wharf in its heyday. Excellent catering facilities - ideal for lunch.
BREWHOUSE ARTS CENTRE - Union Street (fifteen minutes walk from Shobnall Basin). Tel: 01283 516030. Live entertainment, plus attractive bistro/bar.

BUSES - local services throughout the Trent Valley. Tel: 01785 223344.
TRAINS -regular local service to/from Birmingham, Derby & Nottingham. Tel: 08457 484950.

Repton & Willington (Map 19)

A useful watering hole with a trio of cosy pubs, Chinese takeaway, Co-op store, post office and railway station, Willington's real significance lies in its proximity to the ancient settlement of Repton on the far bank of the Trent. Pinpointed by the slender spire of St Wystans, Repton is a worthwhile fifteen minute walk from the canal. The church is of Saxon origin, Repton having been the capital of Mercia in the 9th century until laid waste by marauding Danes. Nowadays the village is best known for its public school. Several good inns and a pleasant farmhouse tearoom can offer refreshment prior to the walk back.

EAST of Burton, the Trent & Mersey doesn't exactly flaunt its freshly acquired widebeam status. True, the bridge-holes are more buxom, but it is not until Stenson Lock is reached, that the true gauge of the canal manifests itself. Barge wide vessels traded upwards from Nottingham to Horninglow until the railways took a grip of the trade in beer; thereafter, even narrowboat traffic dwindled between Fradley and Shardlow. One of the last regular consignments was of cardboard for the manufacture of cigarette papers by Players at Nottingham.

Bridge 31 carries a link road occupying the trackbed of the North Staffordshire Railway's Burton to Tutbury branchline, haunt of a push & pull shuttle known as "The Jinnie". Beyond Stretton the course of the line has become a footpath and nature reserve. Rubber making is a lesser-known facet of the brewery town's economy, though the canalside Pirelli plant has shed much of its workforce in recent times.

Passing over the border between Staffordshire and Derbyshire, marked by an old mill race, the canal crosses the Dove upon a low-slung aqueduct of little aesthetic significance other than the usual invigoration of water spanning water. Beloved of Izaak Walton, the River Dove is virtually

at journey's end here, being less than a mile from its lonely confluence with the Trent at Newton Solney; all a far cry from the glories of Dovedale and the Peak District. An adjacent road bridge, reputedly built by the monks of Burton Abbey, compensates for the aqueduct's plain appearance. On sultry summer days, in spite of dangerous whirlpools, local youths swim in this reach of the Dove.

An imposing Georgian wharf house overlooks Bridge 26 and the site of Egginton's old village wharf. Otherwise the canal is largely featureless as it makes its way through the Trent Valley, as if handcuffed by the portly escorts of a busy dual-carriageway and a main line railway. A pleasant ridge dominates the southern horizon, leading to the stiletto-fine spire of Repton church.

WILLINGTON, a commuter village dominated by an about to be demolished power station, sets its stall out to attract canal visitors. The site of an old rail/canal transhipment wharf has been landscaped and a car park provided for motorists - full of sleeping reps on the occasion of our last visit!

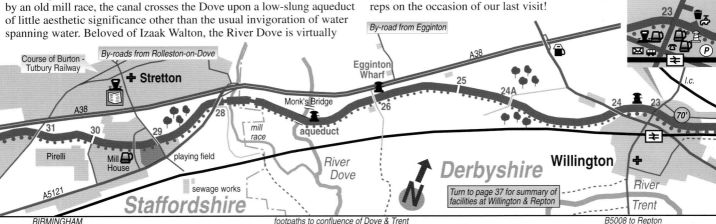

Course of Burton - Tutbury Railway
By-roads from Rolleston-on-Dove
By-road from Egginton
Stretton
Monk's Bridge
Egginton Wharf
A38
A38
mill race
aqueduct
Pirelli
Mill House
playing field
sewage works
River Dove
Derbyshire
Willington
River Trent
Staffordshire
Turn to page 37 for summary of facilities at Willington & Repton
A5121
18
31 30 29 28 26 25 24A 24 23
70'
l.c.
23
P

BIRMINGHAM
footpaths to confluence of Dove & Trent
B5008 to Repton

ARGUABLY at its most prosaic, the Trent & Mersey makes its way between Willington and Swarkestone with the world-weary demeanour of a man who has walked the same dog around the same municipal park twice a day for a dozen years. Intermittent trains break the monotony, but if your adrenalin doesn't flow at the thought of a 'fifty-eight' thrumming by with a payload of slack from what's left of the Nottinghamshire coalfield, then it's time to go below and make the bacon sandwiches. King Coal may be dead - or at least dying - long live King Toyota, now the backbone of the Derbyshire economy. The company's huge plant, masked by the brow of a hill, occupies much of the site of Derby's long lost municipal airport alongside the A38 beyond the village of Findern.

STENSON is well known in boating circles for its large mooring basin, deep wide-beam lock, and a trip boat called *The Bubble*.

Between Stenson and Swarkestone the canal, arm in arm with a railway line used chiefly by goods trains avoiding the centre of Derby, slinks furtively through fields given over to vegetable growing. The feeling that one is a long way from anywhere is misleading. Derby lies just over the rim of the northern horizon. Even closer is the busy A50 trunk road, which serves as a link between the M1 and M6 motorways. But then canals have a knack of conjuring a stimulating sense of isolation in the most unpromising of circumstances.

From Bridge 18, footpaths lead over arable fields to the forgotten Trentside village of Twyford. Once there was a ferry here and the posts which held the chain still stand. We have in our collection an archive photograph of the ferry. Flat-decked, fine-bowed and fairly wide of beam, it is being worked across with the aid of a fixed chain and the river's residual current. A man and boy are occupied with the machinations of the chain whilst two long-skirted ladies - one in a straw bonnet - hold the reins of a horse and trap. Perhaps they were on their way to Repton for groceries. Frozen for posterity, they represent a pace of life obliterated by the development of road transport; and so, on your archaic boat, do you...

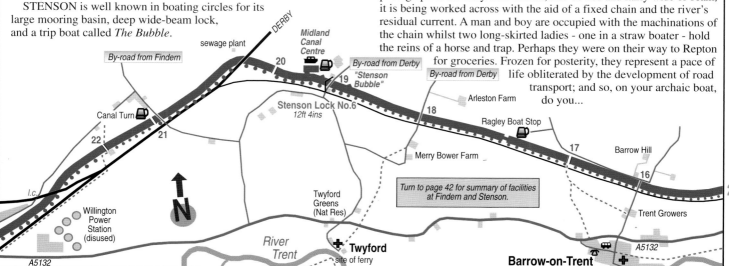

Turn to page 42 for summary of facilities at Findern and Stenson.

NEVER more than half a mile away from the Trent, and often closer, the canal travels through mellow countryside, much of which is given over to market-gardening.

Evidence of occupation by the Beaker People sixteen hundred years before the birth of Christ suggests that man's influence on Swarkestone goes a long way back. Swarkestone Bridge is of relatively modern origin, dating back only to the 12th century. It is generally regarded as the longest stone-built bridge in Britain. In 1347 the scale of tolls quoted charges of a ha'penny for a cask of sturgeons. In 1745 this was the furthest south that Bonnie Prince Charlie's army got in their attempt to capture the throne of England. Just twenty-five years later the Trent & Mersey was being dug, and soon afterwards Swarkestone became the site of a junction with the Derby Canal, including a branch down to the river which only survived until around 1800.

The Derby Canal, overlooked by nationalisation in 1947, was acrimoniously abandoned in 1964, though trade had ceased twenty years earlier. The company who owned the canal were well aware that more money could be made from property deals than from running a public waterway. The old junction house remains intact, used, like the one at Huddlesford on the Coventry Canal, by a local boat club. The Derby Canal's towpath has been resurfaced as part of the Derby Cycle Route and there are ambitious plans to restore at least part of the canal (which linked with the Erewash Canal at Sandiacre) to navigable standard.

By Weston Cliffs the canal glides through tumbling woodland. While construction of the canal was proceeding eastwards, a wharf was erected here for the transfer of goods from barge to riverboat. Later it was used for the transhipment of gypsum bound from Aston to King's Mills, whereupon, after being ground, the resultant plaster was despatched back continued on page 42

Course of Derby Canal & Derby Cycle Route

A514 from Derby

Swarkestone Stop

S.B.C.

Swarkestone Lock No.5
10ft 11ins

Course of Derby & Ashby Railway

15 70' 14

Course of former link with Trent

13

Cuttle Bridge

A5132 from Willington

20

Derby Cycle Route

12

Swarkestone

Hall

ruin

River Trent

Swarkestone Bridge

Sailing Club

N

Stanton by Bridge

A514 to Swadlincote

Course of Derby & Ashby Railway

viaduct

viaduct

site of Bridging School

Derby Cycle Route
(Melbourne 1 mile)

70'

11

site of Military Railway depot

Weston Cliffs

10

former wharf

9

Cooper's Arms

Weston-on-Trent

Old Plough

By-road from Aston-on-Trent

Weston Grange

7

8

Weston Lock No.4
10ft 11ins

Derbyshire

site of lock

site of ferry

King's Mills

Leics.

River Trent

By-road to Castle Donington

2

Gate paddle surge, Swarkestone Lock

continued from page 40

up the canal for consignment via Swarkestone and the Derby Canal to a building merchant in Derby. In these days of the ubiquitous lorry, the amazing complexity and labour-intensiveness of previous eras of transport is mind-boggling.

During the Second World War this dreamy riparian landscape was rudely awakened by the construction of an army camp at Weston Cliffs. It was built to house the army's railway engineers who operated the Melbourne and Ashby line as a military railway during the Second World War. The army camp also provided accommodation for soldiers attached to a Bridging School opened across the river at King's Newton. As part of their training they built a now vanished suspension bridge across the river to facilitate access between the camp and the school. The enigmatic remains of a steam crane used by the bridge-makers remains by the handsome cast-iron railway viaduct which now carries the Derby Cycle Route across the Trent near Bridge 11. The trackbed of that line has been imaginatively resurfaced to create a traffic-free link between Derby and the handsome old market town of Melbourne.

Hardly had the railway engineers marched away, before the camp was commandeered to house Ukrainian refugees. Several hundred arrived here to escape oppression in their homeland in 1944. Weston Rectory, visible on its low hilltop to the north of the canal, was used as a home for the centre's elderly residents, whilst parts of the camp were used by Ukrainian youth groups. A number of Ukrainian children were accommodated here following the Chernobyl nuclear disaster.

The lane from Bridge 8, by Weston Lock, provides easy access to Weston village in one direction. In the other it offers a peaceful walk down to the site of an old lock opposite King's Mills, a popular bathing spot until demolition of a weir in 1957 rendered such activities dangerous. Rummage in the undergrowth and you may discern the remains of the old lock. In the past there was a ferry here too, providing access to the mills on the Leicestershire bank of the Trent - sadly it is no more.

Findern (*Map 20*)

Findern village lies over the horizon and has little to make the walk worthwhile other than a village green.
CANAL TURN - Bridge 21. A busy Ansells pub popular with motorists and boaters alike. Nice big garden and childrens' play area. Tel: 01283 702178.

Stenson (*Map 20*)

A well known canal centre with barn-conversion pub called the STENSON BUBBLE (Tel: 01283 703113). Walk down to Twyford and work up an appetite.

Barrow-on-Trent (*Map 20*)

Barrow's village shop has gone the way of many. RAGLEY BOAT STOP is a family pub converted from an old farm house. Customer moorings are provided on the opposite side to the towpath and water and electricity are laid on for boating patrons. Nice garden, extensive menu. Tel: 01332 703919.

Swarkestone (*Map 21*)

Trent-side village featuring the CREWE & HARPUR (Tel: 01332 700641), a country inn serving bar meals all day, but no shopping facilities other than a garage on the A514. Ruined pavilion associated with long demolished hall visible in fields to the south of the canal.

Weston-on-Trent (*Map 21*)

The second Weston-on-Trent that the Trent & Mersey meets on its travels - the other one's on Map 12 near Stone. No longer has a shop but there are two good pubs:
COOPERS ARMS - Weston Hall. Charming pub housed in 17th century mansion used by Cromwell as a temporary barracks. During the First World War an escaped German prisoner hid here briefly before eventually making his way back to his homeland. Bass beers and a wide choice of food. Tel: 01332 690002.
OLD PLOUGH - traditional village centre pub with a popular restaurant offering an extensive menu including vegetarian options. Tel: 01332 700331.

Shardlow (*Map 22*)

Attractive Georgian village much quieter now that the new A50 has siphoned off the heavy traffic that used to plague its main street. Shardlow Hall was built in 1684 by Leonard Forsbrook from profits made on the river trade. Interesting Heritage Centre on London Road. Tel: 01332 792935.
CLOCK WAREHOUSE - adjacent lock. Mansfield Brewery's vast and imposing warehouse refurbishment popular with families. Lots of good canal archive pictures adorn the walls. Tel: 01332 792844.
MALT SHOVEL - CAMRA recommended traditional pub offering good lunches and Marston's beers. Tel: 01332 792392.
LADY IN GREY - Bridge 2. Stylish restaurant ideal for rewarding tired and morale-sapped crews. Tel: 01332 792331. Other pubs as well plus Tandoori restaurant near church. Shopping facilities limited to a small general store - more gifts than groceries.

NAVIGATION from the Trent to the Mersey must have seemed like a proclamation for travel from the earth to the moon, but this was how the fledgling canal company advertised its purpose back in 1780. The words adorn the largest warehouse at SHARDLOW, the company's 'inland port', once known waggishly as "Rural Rotterdam". And Shardlow, unlike its counterpart Preston Brook, at the other end of the Trent & Mersey, has been fortunate enough to retain the greater part of its historic infrastructure. Pride of place goes to the handsome Clock Warehouse, now a popular pub, alongside Shardlow Lock. Like many of Shardlow's warehouses, it owes its survival to F.E. Stevens, a local animal feeds merchant, whose occupation of this, and several other canalside buildings, secured a use for them in the century which passed between the cessation of the local canal trade and a new era of refurbishment for leisure and commercial use.

Although it is Shardlow which appears on the distinctive Trent &

Mersey mileposts, the actual junction with the Trent Navigation is at Derwent Mouth, approximately one and a half miles east of the village. It's a short journey, as easily accomplished on foot as afloat, for a footpath follows a navigable reach of the Trent back upstream from Derwent Mouth to Cavendish Bridge, creating a three mile walk of intriguing contrast between man-made and natural waterway. An imposing concrete horse-bridge, emblazoned with the initials of the Trent Navigation and dated 1932, carries the towpath across the Trent opposite its confluence with the Derwent. The latter looks alluring, but has not been navigable since the late eighteenth century. Downstream the Trent sweeps haughtily towards Nottingham, an eye-opener for boaters passing through Derwent Mouth Lock and away from the cosy world of the canals. A mile to the east lies Sawley Bridge Marina with its extensive facilities.

But that, as they say, is another story and one that is comprehensively covered in our *East Midlands Canal Companion*. For now you must wend your way back with us along that Trentside footpath beside the uppermost navigable reach of the river, before returning by road to the Trent & Mersey Canal at Shardlow. One of those hurrying cars could get you to Preston Brook in a couple of hours, whereas a boat would take four or five days. But then that's not the point is it!

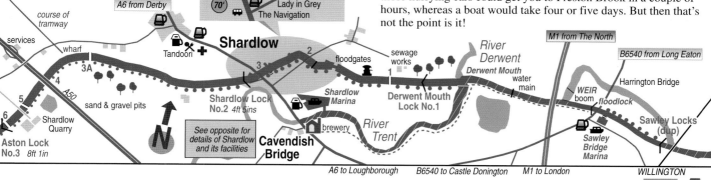

43

MILFORD No 105 BRIDGE

IW(S)AA WATERS MEMBERS ONLY

PATHFINDER J.M. & E.M. GREENHALGH

Milford Bridge, Staffordshire & Worcestershire Canal

LARGELY unmolested, the canal slips quietly through the outskirts of Stafford. The county town stood an aloof mile to the west of the Staffs & Worcs Canal which, in true Brindley fashion, followed the easy contours of the Penk Valley. Plans to construct a branch were dropped in favour of a simple lock down into the Sow, the river being dredged and realigned to take boats as far as a terminal basin at Green Bridge in the centre of Stafford. The navigation was opened in 1816 and in use until the end of the First World War. A footpath follows the riverbank into the town, but it's difficult to imagine how seventy foot narrowboats ever got up there!

Baswich church once stood as isolated on its hillside as Acton Trussell's does still, but now it is surrounded by a housing development, though those with an interest in ecclesiastical architecture can easily reach it from Bridge 100. Note the spelling of the village's name with a 'k' on the bridgeplate. There was a substantial wharf by Radford Bridge, but its site is now somewhat less interestingly occupied by a car showroom following demolition of the original warehouses in the Philistine Seventies.

Stafford Boat Club - with their impressive club house - occupy a former brickworks arm near Hazelstrine Bridge. Most of the works'

output was despatched by canal. Bridge 97 has disappeared completely, there being not even any tell-tale narrowing in the canal's channel where it once must have stood. Hereabouts the inherent other-worldliness of the waterway undergoes strange, paradoxical fluctuations in fortune. Nowhere could be more apparently remote than Deptmore Lock, where the reclusive inhabitant of the rose-clad cottages commutes to the outside world by dinghy. Elsewhere, however, the M6 threatens to intrude like an unwelcome caller on your afternoon off; whilst Acton Trussell, which you'd expect with such a name to be a picture book English village, disappoints with its banal modern architecture. Similarly Wildwood, which ought to be the home of friendly, furry little creatures straight out of some children's tale, has become a housing estate on a hill. But when vapours rise off the Penk, and its marshy meadows ooze sponge-like with excess water, a return to an older, more elemental existence seems somehow tangible, and man's scars upon the landscape recede into the mists of time.

Acton's houses attract a following of ducks. The solitary building on the towpath side used to be a boatman's pub. Present day boaters, however, slake their thirst in the old moated house by Bridge 92, opened a few years ago as a bar and restaurant set in charming grounds. It is said that Brindley actually used the old house's moat for a few yards when building the canal - anything for an easy life.

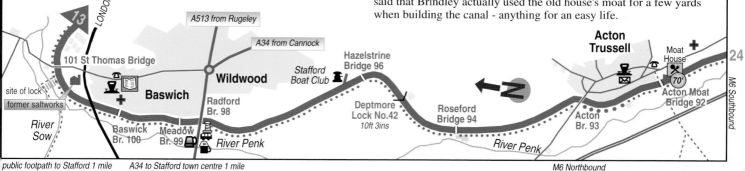

public footpath to Stafford 1 mile   A34 to Stafford town centre 1 mile   M6 Northbound

Penkridge Lock, Staffs & Worcs Canal

Stafford (Map 23)

One of England's lesser-known county towns, Stafford has always seemed too self-effacing for its own good, yet it's a dignified town which hosts some fine public buildings. Unfortunately, for canal folk, the centre lies over a mile from Radford Bridge, but with time at your disposal you could catch one of the frequent buses (Arriva services 1 or 3) and be in town in no time at all. Your first stop should be the Ancient High House in Greengate Street - the main thoroughfare - which houses a Tourist Information desk. Dating from 1595 it's thought to be the largest timber-framed town house remaining in England. Inside there's a heritage exhibition tracing Stafford's history since 913 when Ethelfleda, daughter of Alfred the Great, fortified the settlement against marauding Danish invaders. King Charles I stayed at the High House in 1642 whilst, in later years, Izaak Walton visited relatives who owned it. A town trail leaflet is available to lead you round the best of Stafford's surprisingly rich roll-call of historic buildings.

THE SOUP KITCHEN - Church Lane. Tel: 01785 254775. Quaint, sprawling eating house: coffees, lunches and teas.

STAFFORD ARMS - Railway Street. Back street pub notable for dispensing North Staffordshire brewed Titanic ales. Food and accommodation. Tel: 01785 253313.

RADFORD BANK - canalside Bridge 98. All-day family pub and steak bar. Tel: 01785 242825.

THE MOAT HOUSE - Bridge 92 at Acton Trussell. Highly recommended, family run conversion from moated farmhouse into bar, restaurant and hotel. Beautiful setting, excellent food. Tel: 01785 712217.

Good shopping centre featuring all the well known chain stores plus many attractive individual shops. Good market on Tue, Thur, Fri & Sat. If you have to pass straight by, there are handy local shops at Baswich accessible from bridges 100 and 101. Acton Trussell also has a general store.

TOURIST INFORMATION - Greengate, Stafford, Tel: 01785 240204.

BUSES - services throughout the area. Tel: 0845 705 6005 or 01785 223344.

TRAINS - important railhead. Useful links with Penkridge and Rugeley for towpath walkers. Tel: 08457 484950.

Penkridge (Map 24)

An immediately likeable little town and an excellent place to break your journey. Five minutes walk will take you to the narrow main street, a pleasant spot to shop and saunter. At its foot, beyond the busy A449, stands an impressive church of sandstone, formerly a collegiate church, considered second only to a cathedral in ecclesiastical status. With bicycles at your disposal you might find a ride out on the Brewood road to Cuttlestone Bridge worthwhile.

CROSS KEYS - canalside Bridge 84. A once isolated pub, described by Rolt in Narrow Boat, but now engulfed by housing, though that doesn't diminish its popularity with canallers and motorists alike. Tel: 01785 712826.

THE BOAT - canalside Bridge 86. Attractively refurbished pub overlooking Penkridge Lock. Nice signboard depicting (somewhat inappropriately) an oil tanker barge - presumably escaped from the Aire & Calder! Ansells, Marston's and Morland ales. Good food except for Sunday evenings. Tel: 01785 714178.

More pubs, fish & chips etc in the village centre.

Some lovely little shops of character plus a Co-op supermarket. Lloyds and Barclays banks on A449. Thriving outdoor market beside the river Penk on Wednesdays and Saturdays.

BUSES - to Cannock, Wolverhampton and Stafford. Tel: 01785 223344.

TRAINS - to Wolverhampton and Stafford. Tel: 08457 484950.

A S the canal ascends to (or descends from) its summit level, the locks come thick and fast. The motorway retreats, only to be replaced by the housing estates which cling-wrap the otherwise agreeable little town of Penkridge. Yet, a mile on either side, the countryside is characterised by rolling farmland lifting to the bulwark of Cannock Chase.

The towpath between bridges 90 and 86 is hi-jacked by the "Staffordshire Way" which seems forever to be bumping into canals and appropriating towpaths in the course of its 92 mile journey from Mow Cop to Kinver Edge. Its route has come down off The Chase and crossed Teddesley Park. Teddesley Hall was the seat of Sir Edward Littleton, one of the chief promoters of the Staffordshire & Worcestershire Canal. Indeed, the family remained involved with the canal company until its nationalisation in 1947. The hall itself was demolished by the army in the mid Fifties (having been used as a prison camp for German officers during the Second World War) but the estate farm remains, hidden from the canal by some woodland known as Wellington Belt in commemoration of a visit to the hall by the Iron Duke. Bridge 89 once had ornate balustrades commensurate with its importance as the gateway to the hall, but sadly these have been infilled by brickwork.

PENKRIDGE WHARF is quieter than of late, no longer being the location of a busy boat hire base. Boats still pause here to take on water, however, and there is usually room to moor up for a visit to the town. The Littletons had fingers in many pies, not least the local colliery, which at one time employed over a thousand men. A huge basin, now covered by the motorway, was constructed to enable boats to be loaded with coal from a raised pier by gravity. The chief traffic flow of Littleton coal by canal in later years was down to Stourport power station.

Rodbaston Lock had a keeper until the motorway was built. A special bridge was built over the new road to maintain access to his lockside cottage, but the noise of the ensuing traffic was so bad as to cause him to leave and find new accommodation, the cottage subsequently being demolished. West of the canal between Otherton and Rodbaston lies a college of agriculture.

Map labels:

By-road from Cannock
Rodbaston Br.80
25
site of level crossing
site of coly basin
Rodbaston Lock No.35 8ft 6ins
Otherton Lane Br.81
Otherton Br.82
Otherton Lock No.36 10ft 3ins
Otherton Boat Haven
c'rse of former colliery railway
Lynehill Bridge 83
B5012 from Cannock
Filance Lock No.37 10ft 3ins
sch
Filance Br.84
83A
A449 to Wolverhampton
WOLVERHAMPTON
Longford Lock No.39 10ft 0ins
70'
86
Princefield Br.85
Penkridge Lock No.38 9ft 3ins
Broom Br.87
Teddesley Park Br.89
sch
Penkridge
Longford Bridge 88
River Penk
market
viaduct
A449 from Stafford
STAFFORD
By-road to Brewood
Teddesley Boat Co. Park Gate Br.90
Park Gate Lock No.40 7ft 6ins
Shutt Hill Lock No.41 6ft 0ins
By-road from Brocton
Shutt Hill Br. 91
23
M6 Northbound

CALF HEATH is a strangely isolated tract of country, pancake flat and crossed by a grid of sullen little roads, with here and there a huddle of houses, gathered reassuringly together like something out of Van Gogh's early potato field paintings. The canal all but boxes the compass of this gravel pit-riddled landscape, so that the Chase with its communications tower and the chemical works with its phalanx of flaring chimneys, appear to move about you, teasing you into geographic insecurity, like a game of Blind Man's Buff.

The Staffs & Worcs Canal's summit lies at more or less 340 feet above sea level. Industry lines the canal at Four Ashes. The old tar works here was once served by Thomas Clayton boats.

The last load of Cannock coal came off the Hatherton Branch in 1949 and it was abandoned a couple of years later. However, the illusion of a junction remains, because the bottom lock (of what was once a flight of eight in three miles) is still used to provide access to moorings. A preservation group is actively seeking restoration of the branch with the intention of linking it with the northern waters of the BCN at Norton Canes. Much work would be involved, but it is difficult to think of a more worthwhile restoration scheme in the context of the midland canal network.

Watling Street crosses the canal at Gailey. The most significant feature here is the 'round house', originally a toll clerk's office but now a splendid canal shop run by mother and daughter team, Eileen and Karen Lester. There is something spellbinding about cylindrical buildings - Martello towers, windmills, lighthouses; even Birmingham's Bull Ring Rotunda - and Gailey round house, in its lock-side setting, has a particular charm which you will want to try and capture on film.

Map labels

A5 from London

Course of Hatherton Branch

Gailey Reservoirs

HATHERTON JUNCTION

Calf Heath Marina

Hatherton Marina

Calf Heath

M6

12

Calf Heath Reservoir

Bogg's Lock No.34 8ft 6ins

Brick Kiln Lock No.33 8ft 6ins

A5 "Watling Street"

70'

Long Moll's Bridge 76

Deepmore Bridge 75

70'

26

gravel pits

70'

Four Ashes

Gailey Wharf
Gailey Lock No.32 8ft 6ins

79

Viking Afloat
J.D.Boat Services

Calf Heath Bridge 77

Roundhouse Canal Shop

Gravelley Way Br.78

chemical works

Stafford - Wolverhampton

A449

24

Summary of Facilities

GAILEY ROUND HOUSE is one of the most charming canal gift shops on the system. A modest range of provisions is usually available. There is a good general store half a mile west of Gailey Wharf where the A5 crosses the A449.

THE canal exchanges the loneliness of Calf and Coven heaths for the industrial and suburban outskirts of Wolverhampton; the M54 to Telford forming an obvious, though not intentional, boundary. At Cross Green a former canal pub called "The Anchor" has become a popular steak bar and many boaters choose to moor here overnight. As it passes beneath the M54 the canal crosses the county boundary between Staffordshire and the West Midlands, one of the new counties which had its origins in the local government changes of 1974. Many people still mourn the old counties. It must have been galling, for instance, to have lived in Lincolnshire all one's life and wake up one morning in South Humberside. West Midlands was possibly the dullest of all the new names, and sounds as though it must have been the compromise of a committee. Black Country would have been a far more appropriate and resonant title. You can imagine its inhabitants espousing a perverse pride in such a name, no-one could possibly show a flicker of interest in anyone who admitted to coming from the West Midlands!

The most significant feature of this length is "Pendeford Rockin", the old boatmen's name for a shallow, but tellingly narrow cutting hewn by Brindley's navvies through a solid belt of sandstone which breaks through the clay strata at this point. The cutting, half a mile or so long, restricts the channel to such a degree that you begin to wonder if you have lost concentration and taken a wrong turn. There are, however, one or two passing places - as on a single lane road - where oncoming boats can be successfully negotiated without losing one's temper. Similar narrows occur on the Shropshire Union north of Autherley as that canal encounters the same difficult rock.

West Midlands

A449 to Wolverhampton

Staffordshire

74 Moat House Bridge

73 The Laches Bridge

Coven Heath

2

'Pendeford Rockin' NARROWS!

school

27

Brinsford Bridge 70

70'

70'

golf club

72 Slade Heath Bridge

71 Cross Green Bridge

The Anchor

sewage wks

69 Coven Heath Bridge

Forster Bridge 68

Marsh Lane Bridge 67

M54 to Telford

By-road to Codsall

Coven

A449 to Stafford

To Brewood

Summary of Facilities

Coven's village centre is less than ten minutes walk from Bridge 71 - but take care crossing the A449. Facilities include a post office, general store, grocer, butcher, bakery, newsagent and fish & chip shop. Canalside you'll find THE ANCHOR steak bar - Tel: 01902 790466. Alternatively you could try the local golf club restaurant or bistro where visitors are welcome - adjacent Bridge 71. There's an hourly bus service to/from Wolverhampton.

Shropshire Union Canal

Sunlight and shadow in a typical 'Shroppie' cuttir

DESPITE the proximity of Wolverhampton, Autherley, like many canal junctions, is self-contained. It is not pretty in a conventional sense, being bordered by housing estates, sewage plants and public open spaces. In typically pithy fashion, the old boatmen called it 'Cut End', for the obvious reason that the Shropshire Union Canal began and, more pertinently, ended here. Once there was all the paraphernalia of a meeting of waterways: toll office, stables, workshops, employees cottages, and a dominant, sweeping roving bridge carrying the Staffs & Worcs towpath over the entrance to the Shropshire Union. A stop lock - just six inches deep - protected the two companies' precious water supplies. Much of this infrastructure survives, enjoying a new lease of life in the leisure age as a hire base and boatyard.

A massive sewage plant provides the canal with much of its water; suitably treated of course, or perhaps this explains the Shropshire Union's apparent impatience to get on with its journey to the north-west. Whatever the motivation, Autherley is soon forgotten as the canal crosses the boundary between the West Midlands and Staffordshire and leaves the housing estates of suburban

Wolverhampton behind. The land east of the canal was once occupied by an aerodrome, whilst the works by Bridge 4 was formerly an aircraft factory, turning out, amongst other designs, the 'Defiant' fighter plane.

An 'invisible' aqueduct carries the canal over the little River Penk before the waterway goes through a series of contortions which see it narrowing, then widening, then narrowing again before resuming its usual width beyond Bridge 6. Jonathan Morris, a former lock-keeper, theorised in his detailed towpath guide to the canal that the narrow sandstone cuttings were cost-cutting exercises, brought about by cash-flow difficulties as the canal was being built. The wider pool beyond Bridge 5 - known locally as 'The Hattons' or 'figure o'three' - he suggests, related to former clay workings done on site as it were. The M54 intrudes a moment of modern reality, but otherwise the landscape is peacefully rural, setting the scene for the forty mile journey to Nantwich through some unexpectedly remote countryside.

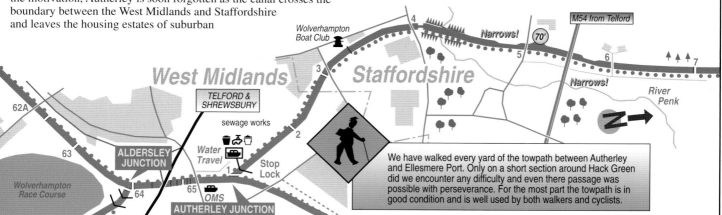

Wolverhampton Boat Club

West Midlands

Staffordshire

4

Narrows! (70')

M54 from Telford

5

6

7

28

3

TELFORD & SHREWSBURY

sewage works

62A

Water Travel

63

ALDERSLEY JUNCTION

2

Narrows!

River Penk

1

Stop Lock

65

OMS

We have walked every yard of the towpath between Autherley and Ellesmere Port. Only on a short section around Hack Green did we encounter any difficulty and even there passage was possible with perseverance. For the most part the towpath is in good condition and is well used by both walkers and cyclists.

Wolverhampton Race Course

64

AUTHERLEY JUNCTION

Birmingham Canal to Wolverhampton

To Wolverhampton

26

THE Shropshire Union slices through the Staffordshire countryside in cuttings and upon embankments typical of the bold, 19th century designs of Thomas Telford, who engineered this route between Autherley and Nantwich, originally known as the Birmingham & Liverpool Junction Canal. Travelling northwards you rapidly become attuned to the unique atmosphere of this canal. Far from becoming monotonous, its purposeful, loping stride across the landscape is strangely exhilarating, perhaps due to the recurring contrast of shadowy cuttings and panorama providing embankments, known as 'rockings' and 'valleys' respectively to past generations of boatmen.

There are two notable structures either side of Brewood. To the south the distinctly ornate, balustraded Avenue Bridge (No 10) carries the carriageway to Chillington Hall. The advent of the canals heralded many similar attempts at ornamentation and disguise, where powerful landowners would only condescend to permit a waterway to cross their parklands if suitable steps were taken to adorn the otherwise purely functional architecture of the new trade route. In contrast, north of Brewood, the canal crosses the old Roman Road of Watling Street on a sturdy, yet elegant aqueduct of iron, brick and stone construction. Nearby Belvide Reservoir is one of the main sources of water supply for the Shropshire Union Canal, whilst Broom Hall, east of Bridge 16, was the home of William Carlos who hid King Charles II in the oak tree at nearby Boscobel after the Battle of Worcester in 1651.

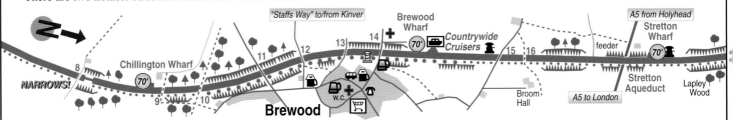

BREWOOD

A lovely village, retaining an ancient air of calm. The natives call it 'Brood', and there really is a timelessness about it which seduces you into spending longer here than you might have planned. Winding lanes of gracious houses lead to the old market place where the distinctive vehicles of the Green Bus Company pause before rumbling off to Wolverhampton. Enhancing one corner of the square is 'Speedwell Castle', a Gothic fantasy erected in the 18th century on the winnings of a racehorse named Speedwell.

CONNOISSEUR TEA ROOMS - corner of the Square. Morning coffee, lunches, afternoon teas; plus dinner menu selected evenings. Tel: 01902 851694.
ADMIRAL RODNEY - Dean Street. Tel: 01902 850583. Les Routiers recommended pub with good choice of food.
BRIDGE INN - Bridge 14. Much extended former boatmans' pub. Burtonwood beers. Tel: 01902 850778.
Old fashioned shops where you can eavesdrop on local gossip: baker, butcher, chemist, newsagent with post office counter, small supermarket and branch of Lloyds TSB Bank. Calor gas from garage by Bridge 14. COOPERS foodstore is excellent.
CHILLINGTON HALL - Georgian House with 'Capability Brown gardens' located just over a mile west of Bridge 10. Open Thursday afternoons in summer. Admission charge. Tel: 01902 850397.
BUSES - Frequent Green Bus Co services (Mon-Sat) to/from Wolverhampton; some run through to/from Wheaton Aston and are thus useful for one-way towpath walks. Tel: 01922 414141.

WHEATON ASTON Lock is strangely solitary - the only one in 25 miles of canal; a telling statistic of Telford's engineering. For about a mile the canal penetrates the deciduous heart of Lapley Wood, and there's another typical Shroppie cutting by Little Onn, but elsewhere the embankments offer wide views eastwards towards Cannock Chase.

How astonishingly remote and unpeopled the landscape seems. The West Midlands conurbation is less than a dozen miles to the south, yet moor for the night between Wheaton Aston and Little Onn, and you'll have only the occasional eerie hoot of a hunting owl, or the distant silent wash of headlights on a country lane, for company.

Abandoned wartime aerodromes inevitably have their ghosts, and in decay accumulate a patina of lore and legend, hard perhaps to equate with the often mundane use to which they were put after closure. Wheaton Aston was opened in 1941 and became one of the RAF's largest training units, operating a squadron of 'Oxfords'. There were at least two canal dramas. Once an American 'Thunderbolt' crash-landed in the waterway. Another well remembered wartime incident occurred at the lock when a narrowboat, carrying an unsheeted cargo of shining aluminium on a moonlit night, was attacked by a German aircraft which unleashed a bomb that exploded less than a hundred yards from the chamber. Swords into ploughshares: after the war the aerodrome became a pig farm!

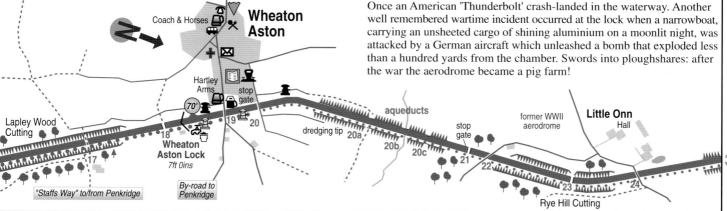

WHEATON ASTON

Once purely a farming community, Wheaton Aston has been completely overwhelmed by modern housing; with its long straggling main street, it's certainly no picture postcard village. Nevertheless, it appears to be thriving, defying the trend towards rural decline, and a good range of shops makes it a useful port of call for the Shroppie boater.

LA CALVADOS - Main Street. French restaurant open Tue-Sat for dinner and for Sunday lunch. Tel: 01785 840707 for bookings.
HARTLEY ARMS - canalside Bridge 19. Popular pub offering a good range of food. Tel: 01785 840232.
COACH & HORSES - village centre. Old fashioned Banks's local. Tel: 01785 841048.

Post office, general stores, baker, butchers, newsagents and greengrocers all within 5 minutes' walk of Bridge 19. Turner's canalside garage stocks Calor gas, diesel and boating accessories.
BUSES - Services to/from Brewood, Wolverhampton, Penkridge and Cannock. Tel: 01785 223344.

*T*HE buildings of two wharves remain intact at High Onn. One belonged to Cadbury's, the other to a local landowner, suggesting that there was once a degree of agricultural traffic on the canal.

Deep shadowy sandstone cuttings, spanned by lichened grey stone bridges of simple balance and unaffected beauty, lead to the eighty-one unlined yards of Cowley Tunnel; the only one on the Shropshire Union. Once a dizzy jungle of trees darkened the approaches so much that you were never quite sure where the tunnel began and the cutting ended, but their roots caused instabilities in

what was already a brittle rock strata and they were felled in 1985.

On a clear day the embankments north of Gnosall reveal that famous Shropshire landmark, The Wrekin, 15 miles to the south-west; a slumbering hunchback of a summit, 1335ft high. A.E.Housman celebrated it in *A Shropshire Lad,* and Salopians raise their glasses in a toast to: "All friends around the Wrekin".

The dismantled railway line which crossed the canal at Gnosall once usefully connected Stafford with Shrewsbury until a certain doctor made his presence felt. Historically it was unusual in that it was actually built by the Shropshire Union Canal Company, apparently hedging their bets on the transport mode of the future. When, in 1846, they leased themselves to the London & North Western Railway, few shareholders would have backed the canal to outlast the railway as it has done.

former Cadbury milk depot
Lord Talbot's Wharf
well
70'
29
25 26 27 28
Joan Eaton's Cross
By-road to Church Eaton
Chamberlain's Covert
29 30
Home Farm
31 32
Cowley Tunnel No.33
Gnosall Heath
A518 to Gnosall & Stafford
The Boat
34 35
35A 36
A518 from Newport
former flour mill
Millennium Way (Course of Stafford - Shrewsbury railway)
37

GNOSALL HEATH

This appendage of Gnosall (No-zull) grew up with the coming of the canal. Two pubs slaked the thirst of passing boatmen, a steam powered flour mill took advantage of the new transport mode, and a non-conformist chapel kept a sense of proportion amidst all the excitement. Nowadays the pubs pander to pleasure boaters and passing motorists, the flour mill has become a private residence, and the chapel is a hardware store. Few boaters take the trouble to visit Gnosall itself, half a mile to the east, though it has a lovely church.

THE BOAT - Bridge 34. Marston's pub with attractive curved wall abutting the bridge. Food available and pleasant garden by the water's edge. Tel: 01785 822208.
THE NAVIGATION - Bridge 35. Nice garden with good children's playground. Tel: 01785 822327.

Fish & chips on A518 open daily (except Sundays), both sessions.
General store/newsagent, butcher & pet shop by Bridge 34. Post office by Bridge 35.
BUSES - services to/from Stafford and Newport. Tel: 01785 223344.

A MASK of tall trees disguises the immensity of Shelmore embankment. It was six years in the making and, in its way, was as glorious an engineering feat as any of Telford's more visibly imposing aqueducts. A vast army of navvies and horses was employed on it. Spoil from the big cuttings at nearby Gnosall and Grub Street was brought by wagon for its construction. To Telford's dismay the earthworks slipped time after time and, as the rest of the canal was finished, Shelmore stubbornly refused to hold. In poor health, Telford struggled to oversee its completion, conscious that the bank need not have been tackled at all, had Lord Anson of Norbury Park sanctioned the preferred course through Shelmore Wood. Perhaps we should regard his lordship more kindly from today's perspective when environmentalists, protecting the landscape from new motorways, are on the side of the angels.

Sadly, Norbury is no longer a junction, though the name lives on. How nice it would be to lock down the 'Seventeen Steps' of the Newport Branch and head across the marshy emptiness of Shropshire's Weald Moors to Shrewsbury.

North of Norbury lies Grub Street cutting. For over a mile the canal is wrapped in a thick coat of vegetation, again, like Shelmore, hiding the sheer size of the eighty foot deep cutting, whose most unusual feature is the double-arched bridge which carries the A519 across the canal. The tiny telegraph pole is a survivor from the line which once marched beside the Shroppie for much of its length. Ironically, canals are again being used as lines of communication with the burying of optical fibres beneath selected lengths of towpath. It is to be hoped that this hi-tech activity meets with the approval of the black, monkey-like creature reputed to have haunted Bridge 39 ever since a boatman was killed here in the 19th century.

Map labels

Course of Newport Branch Canal

Shelmore Embankment

NORBURY JUNCTION

Junction Inn

British Waterways

Anglo Welsh

70' 38

Norbury

A519 from Newport

A519 to Eccleshall

39

Grub Street Cutting

40 41

70'

The Anchor

42 43

By-road to High Offley

32

NORBURY JUNCTION

An atmospheric canal community, and although the suffix is misleading nowadays, Norbury remains a flourishing canal centre where British Waterways have an office and maintenance yard. Some of the houses are still occupied by canal workers, but one is available for holiday accommodation bookable through the boatyard.

JUNCTION INN - canalside Bridge 38. Busy pub now run by Anglo Welsh. Garden with children's play area. Bar and restaurant meals. Tel: 01785 284288. Gift shop in garden.

ANCHOR INN - canalside Bridge 42. Famously unspoilt boatman's pub serving Devizes-brewed Wadworth 6X from the jug. Gift shop to rear selling souvenirs and T-shirts. Tel: 01785 284569.

THE MEASHAM TEAPOT - cosy little adjunct to the boatyard shop. Light meals as available.
Boatyard shop: provisions, off licence, gifts. A truly useful facility between Gnosall and 'Drayton.

CROSSING the border between Staffordshire and Shropshire, the canal continues to traverse an uncluttered countryside almost entirely given over to agriculture. It can come as a surprise to find so remote a landscape in the 'crowded' middle of England. One is tempted to categorise the area as 'lost' but for the obvious truth that it has never been 'found' in the first place.

Blithely we pleasure boaters sail across embankments and through cuttings with no more thought for their construction than if we were driving down the M6. But imagine the impact of Telford's brash new canal on the surrounding early nineteenth century landscape. Put yourself in the position of Sir Richard Whitworth's tenant farmer at Batchacre Park. Up until 1830 dawn rose across the open pasturelands throwing light through his east-facing windows. A year later his view of the rising sun was cut off forever by an embankment twice the height of the farmhouse. No wonder the landowners of this rural corner of Staffordshire had their misgivings, and the canal company paid dearly

in compensation for the land they acquired.

It comes as something of a surprise to encounter a confectionery factory in the midst of otherwise empty countryside. It was opened by Cadbury, the chocolate manufacturers, in 1911 as a centre for processing milk collected from the dairy farming hinterland of the Shropshire Union Canal. Canal transport was used exclusively to bring countless churns gathered from numerous wharves along the canal; from simple wooden stages at the foot of fields, to the sophistication of Cadbury's own plant at High Onn. Cadbury owned a distinctive fleet of narrowboats, being one of the first operators to experiment with motorised craft. Cocoa and sugar crumb were also brought by boat to Knighton and blended with milk to make raw chocolate, itself returned to Bournville, again by boat, to be transformed into the finished delicacy.

The last boatman to trade to Knighton was Charlie Atkins senior; nicknamed 'Chocolate Charlie' for obvious reasons. He carried the final cargo from Knighton to Bournville in 1961. Since then all transport to and from the still busy works has been by road. Attempts to have the handsome Art Deco type canalside buildings demolished have, thus far at least, been staved off by a preservation order.

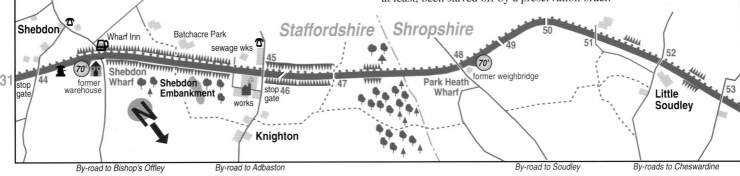

THE Shroppie flirts with the county boundary, the towpath forming the demarcation so that, technically, the canal lies briefly in Staffordshire. The landscape, though, is impervious to the machinations of local government, remaining aloof and typically remote: a tall, dark, silent canal, this Shropshire Union.

WOODSEAVES is another prodigious cutting. The canal narrows and, in places, is cut through solid rock. These cuttings proved just as troublesome to Telford and his contractors as did the embankments. There were frequent avalanches during construction and, even today, brittle lumps of sandstone are inclined to dislodge themselves and tumble into the canal; one reason why a 2mph speed limit is imposed. Walkers will be grateful for the cool shade on hot days - cyclists might find the going tricky. A feature of Woodseaves is its pair of high bridges, spanning the canal like portals to the mysterious chasms of another world.

At TYRLEY a flight of five locks - the last to be faced southbound for seventeen miles - carries the canal down into, or up out of, Market Drayton. The lower chambers are located in a shadowy sandstone cutting across which branches intertwine to form a tunnel of trees. Damp and rarely touched by sunlight, all manner of mosses and ferns flourish in this conducive environment.

After dusk bats leave their tree bole roosts to hunt for insects, acrobatically twisting and turning over the luminous pounds between the locks. The well-surfaced towpath makes the flight popular with pedestrians but parking is restricted on the lane which crosses the canal by bridge 60. The provision of a sanitary station and rubbish point above the top lock satisfies the needs of boaters too.

TYRLEY WHARF was a point of discharge and collection for the local estate at Peatswood. The buildings date from 1837 and were erected in a graceful Tudor style by the local landowner. Nowadays, its commercial significance a thing of the dim and distant past, it would be difficult to imagine a more picturesque scene though it is sad that the craft shop and home-baking outlet, admirable enterprises of the 1980s, have both been and gone.

SUMMARY OF FACILITIES

There are no shops to be found on this length of canal other than by walking a country mile from Goldstone Wharf to Cheswardine; though with names as beautiful as that you could spend the walking time turning a verse or two.
THE WHARF TAVERN (Bridge 55) is one of 'The Shroppie's' most popular pubs, widely regarded for its restaurant meals. Bar food - including an ample summer buffet - is also readily available. There's a spacious canalside garden and a payphone on the premises. Tel: 01630 661226.

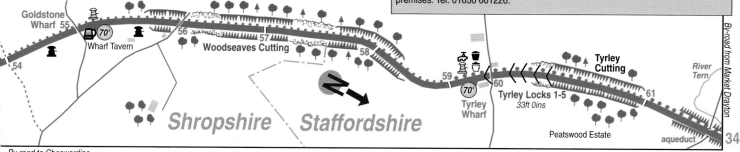

Goldstone Wharf 55 · Wharf Tavern · 54 · 56 · Woodseaves Cutting · 57 · 58 · Shropshire · Staffordshire · By-road to Cheswardine · 59 · 60 · Tyrley Wharf · Tyrley Locks 1-5 33ft 0ins · Peatswood Estate · Tyrley Cutting · 61 · River Tern · aqueduct · By-road from Market Drayton · 34

MARKET DRAYTON was the largest, in fact the only, town encountered by the old Birmingham & Liverpool Junction Canal on its route from Autherley to Nantwich. Naturally, a sizeable wharf was provided for dealing with local cargoes; though the canal's monopoly on local trade lasted only thirty years before the railway reached the town. It is sometimes difficult, in these days of the ubiquitous juggernaut, to appreciate the importance of the canal wharf and the railway goods yard to the past prosperity of small towns like Drayton. They must have been the hub of local life, few businesses would have been able to carry out their trade without regular recourse to the wharfinger and the stationmaster. From the opening of the canal until the First World War no commodity, apart from local agricultural produce, could have arrived at Market Drayton, or been dispatched, without the involvement of these important gentlemen. On the canal a large basin and a sizeable warehouse and adjoining cornmill (refurbished now as a craft shop and antiques centre) remind us of this lost significance.

Pleasant 48 hour moorings, bordered by school playing fields, stretch south from Bridge 62 to the imposing aqueduct over the lane to Peatswood. Steps lead down to the road below, which crosses the little River Tern nearby and forms the most romantic, but not the most convenient, approach to the town centre. South of Bridge 64 a modestly-sized new housing development adjoins the canal and its associated private moorings have 'swallowed up' the turning point once provided here.

BETTON CUTTING is not among 'The Shroppie's' most dramatic, but it is reputed to be haunted by a shrieking spectre, and working boatmen would avoid lingering here in the old days. Indeed, it could be said that this whole canal has something of a fey quality about it, a blurring of past and present which is liable to send shivers down susceptible spines.

Nevertheless, the quiet charm of the countryside continues to impress - unspectacular perhaps, but epitomising 'England's green and pleasant land' to perfection. The ADDERLEY flight is neat and tidy, although not the place it was when every chamber was bordered by flower beds and the grass manicured like a bowling green. A privet hedge beside the third lock down indicates the site of a demolished lock-keeper's cottage, one of many to have disappeared from the canal system over the years.

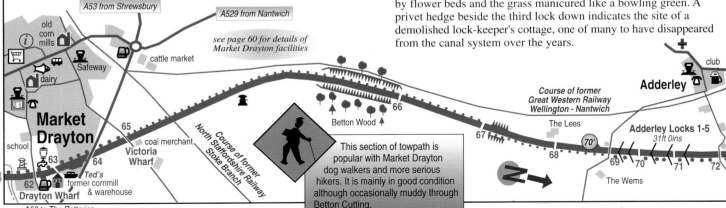

A53 from Shrewsbury

A529 from Nantwich

see page 60 for details of Market Drayton facilities

old corn mills

Safeway

cattle market

dairy

Market Drayton

school

coal merchant

Victoria Wharf

Course of former North Staffordshire Railway Stoke Branch

Betton Wood

Course of former Great Western Railway Wellington - Nantwich

The Lees

Adderley

club

Adderley Locks 1-5
31ft 0ins

The Wems

Ted's former cornmill & warehouse

Drayton Wharf

A53 to The Potteries

This section of towpath is popular with Market Drayton dog walkers and more serious hikers. It is mainly in good condition although occasionally muddy through Betton Cutting.

33

Conversation piece, Betton Mill, Market Drayton

Market Drayton *(Map 34)*

Self-styled as "The Home of Gingerbread", the day to see 'Drayton at its best is Wednesday when the 750 years old market still packs the quaint, narrow streets with stalls and country bumpkins intent on a bargain and a gossip. This gregarious gathering is the town's real heritage, along with its half-timbered town houses which mostly date from the aftermath of a fire which swept through the place in 1651. Market Drayton's most famous son was Robert Clive, best remembered here for scaling the sturdy tower of St Mary's and for blackmailing local shopkeepers. Such youthful escapades proved ideal preparation for a career in diplomacy and military leadership. He established British rule in the Sub Continent and became known as 'Clive of India'.

Drayton bristles with pubs and Marston's beer seems to predominate. Look no further than THE TALBOT (Tel: 01630 661226), a handsome, redbrick Georgian inn just east of Bridge 62. There are a couple of fish & chip shops and an Indian restaurant/takeaway in Shropshire Street.

Safeway, Somerfield and KwikSave must make it difficult for the little shops to survive in a small country town like this, but those that remain put a brave face on it. We were sorry to see that our favourite sweet shop has gone, its premises taken over by an estate agent. The secondhand bookshop is another casualty. By way of consolation notice has at last been taken of the fine old mill by Bridge 63. The ground floor has become the home of WOODIES, an enterprising new - albeit small - craft shop (Tel: 01630 653564) whilst the upper storeys are due to be occupied by an antique dealer. For those 'Flying Dutchmen' among you, doomed to cruise the canals for eternity, there's a launderette in Shropshire Street. Not surprisingly, Billingtons 'original' gingerbread is widely available from a number of food shops - or, in fact, the TIC as well.

(i) TOURIST INFORMATION - Cheshire Street.
Tel: 01630 652139.

BUSES - services to/from Stoke, Shrewsbury and occasionally Audlem.
Tel: 0345 056785

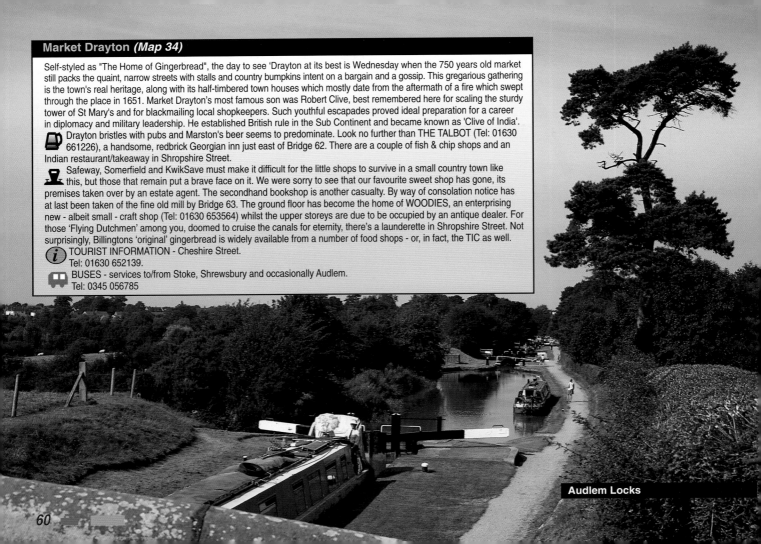

Audlem Locks

60

FIFTEEN locks running through a cutting of larch and Scots pine take the canal across the Shropshire/Cheshire border. The locks are well-maintained and a pleasure to operate. The barrel-roofed building by lock 10 was used by stonemasons, blacksmiths and carpenters engaged in maintaining the flight. Towards the foot of the flight - known to old boatmen as the Audlem "Thick" - you pass Audlem Wharf, one of the prettiest ports of call on the Shropshire Union, with a former warehouse restored as a popular pub and the adjacent lofty mill converted into a superb craft shop.

North of the bottom lock, below which is a well preserved stable block used as a base by the Daystar Theatre Group, the canal, wide with concrete banking but deceptively shallow, bounds across the infant River Weaver on a high embankment. One of the craziest notions of the Ministry of War Transport during the Second World War was to make the Weaver navigable by 100 ton barges to this point, beyond which a lift would carry them up to the level of the Shropshire Union, upgraded sufficiently for them to travel as far south as Wolverhampton. Pleasure boaters can be thankful that this scheme never got off the drawing board and can moor at the foot of the Audlem flight in splendid isolation.

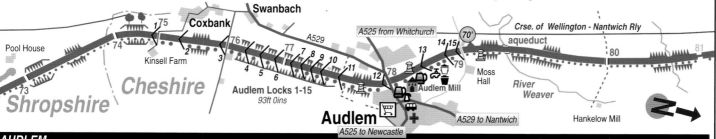

AUDLEM

"The sleepers sleep at Audlem" sang Flanders and Swann in "Slow Train", their elegy for the Beeching cuts, and whilst they were referring to the village's station and its imminent closure, Audlem remains a sleepy place. Now that the trains have gone and the average motorist is hell bent on getting somewhere else as fast as he can, only the canal traveller is journeying at a pace to do justice to this lovely village, highpoints of which are the ancient buttermarket and parish church.

THE BRIDGE - canalside Bridge 78. Unspoilt former boatmans' pub; food.

THE SHROPPIE FLY - canalside Lock 13. Nicely furnished warehouse conversion serving bar and restaurant meals.
THE LORD COMBERMERE - The Square. Popular village local. Food, families welcome.
STAVSONS - Cheshire Street. Fish & chips, pies etc.
OLD PRIESTS HOUSE - The Square. Coffees, teas and light lunches.
KAPAZ PIZZA PARLOUR - Little Italy comes to Cheshire!
BUSES - services to/from Nantwich, Whitchurch, Crewe and Market Drayton (latter Weds only). Tel: 01270 505350.

Friendly shops cater for most needs and make shopping here a pleasure rather than a stressful chore. Many shops indulge in a lunchtime siesta, though, and Wednesday is half-day. Ice cream, made on the premises, is available from the old fashioned confectioners by the market cross. Audlem's outstanding establishment, however, is the AUDLEM MILL CANAL SHOP converted from the three-storey Kingbur mill by John Stothert in 1976. Shopping and browsing here is, in the proprietor's own words: "Just as much a social event as a retail experience."

AT Hack Green there are two isolated locks and the remnants of a stable, recalling the practice of frequent changing of horses on the 'fly' boats which travelled day and night with urgent, perishable cargoes. This is the Cheshire Plain and dairy farming has long been a vital part of the area's economy - though for how much longer one might wonder, given the precarious state of agriculture at the beginning of the 21st century. We tend to think of farming as an unchanging facet of the landscape, but the Friesian cattle synonymous with milk production would have seemed like interlopers to 19th century boatmen more used to indigenous British breeds like Ayrshires and Alderneys.

Unchanging landscape! Thank goodness this is comparatively true, for when we first explored this canal in the early Eighties we were blissfully unaware of Hack Green's nuclear bunker, a Second World War radar station secretly designated to play a role as a Regional Government Headquarters in the event of a nuclear war. Deemed redundant at the end of the Cold War, it has somewhat bizarrely become a tourist attraction:

"a unique and exciting day out for all the family". Fascinating stuff, but more than a little unnerving too.

Adroitly changing the subject, let us recall how trade survived on this canal until the 1960s; which much be some sort of testimony to the viability of canal carrying. Perhaps in the final analysis attitudes rather than economics prevailed. One of the most celebrated traffics on the Shroppie in latter years was Thomas Clayton's oil run from Stanlow on the banks of the Mersey to Langley Green, near Oldbury in the Black Country. The contract commenced in 1924 and the Clayton boats, with their characteristic decked holds, and river names, were a mainstay of trade on the canal for thirty years. Even post-war, a thousand boat-loads per annum were being despatched from Stanlow, some remaining horse-drawn until the early Fifties. But, in common with other canals, the Shropshire Union lost its final freights to the motor lorry; then, for many, with the disappearance of its working boats, something died on the Shroppie, some intangible component of canal heritage that no amount of preservation, nor hectic holiday trade, can ever compensate for.

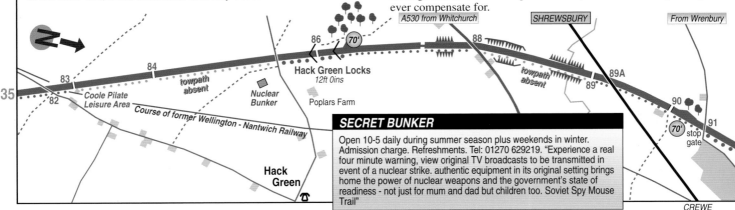

SECRET BUNKER

Open 10-5 daily during summer season plus weekends in winter. Admission charge. Refreshments. Tel: 01270 629219. "Experience a real four minute warning, view original TV broadcasts to be transmitted in event of a nuclear strike. authentic equipment in its original setting brings home the power of nuclear weapons and the government's state of readiness - not just for mum and dad but children too. Soviet Spy Mouse Trail"

THE character of the Shropshire Union Canal changes perceptibly at Nantwich: northwards lie the broad, winding waters of its earlier constituent, the Chester Canal; southwards the direct and narrow Birmingham & Liverpool Junction Canal. A broad embankment elevates the canal above the housing, back gardens and allotments which constitute the periphery of Nantwich. Ironically, these earthworks, together with a cast iron aqueduct over the Chester road, could have been avoided if the owners of Dorfold Hall had not objected to the passage of the canal across their land. The basin and former terminus of the Chester Canal, indicating the more expedient route to the south which Telford would have liked to have used, nowadays provides valuable mooring space, long term and short term, and there is a certain pleasure to be had from manoeuvring in and out of its narrow confines. Adjoining the basin are the premises of the Nantwich & Border Counties Yachting Club. Between Nantwich and Hurleston junction (Map 38) the Chester Canal, dating from 1779, passes uneventfully through a landscape typical of the Cheshire Plain.

NANTWICH

The octagonal tower of St Mary's church, glimpsed across the rooftops from the high canal embankment, tempts you to moor and get to know this picturesque and historic Cheshire town. Walking in from the basin, the aqueduct forms an appropriate portcullis, and the appeal of the town increases as the centre is reached. Few English towns are cleaner or better endowed with floral displays. In medieval times Nantwich was the chief salt producing town in the county. For a brief Victorian heyday it flourished as a spa town.

No shortage here of tea rooms, coaching inns or ethnic restaurants, though all are at least 15 minutes walk from the canal. The nearest pub, THE ODDFELLOWS ARMS on Welsh Row, is little over 5 minutes away, however; and almost opposite is a fish & chip shop offering the option of eating in or taking away.

BUSES - services throughout the area. The Hanley - Chester C84 calls, usefully for towpath treks, at Barbridge. Tel: 01270 505350.
TRAINS - services to/from Crewe and Shrewsbury. Tel: 08457 484950.

More affluent than Whitchurch or Market Drayton, Nantwich's antique shops and boutiques emphasise its position at the centre of a well-heeled hinterland. But it is perhaps the food sellers that are most satisfying: butchers like CLEWLOWS, bakers like CHATWINS and fishmongers like SEA BREEZES all of whom have branches in Pepper Street. A market is held on Thursdays and Saturdays, whilst Wednesday is half day closing. For those (misguidedly!) not making the trek into the town centre, an excellent corner shop, is located on Welsh Row, just five minutes' walk from the aqueduct. Laundry facilities are available at the canal basin.

TOURIST INFORMATION - Church Walk. Tel: 01270 610983.
NANTWICH MUSEUM - Well presented displays of local history. Free admission. Tel: 01270 827104.

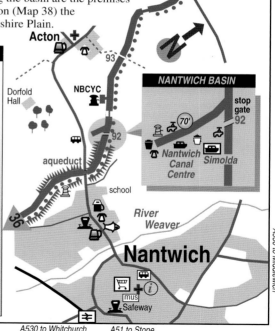

96
38
Henhull Moorings 70'
95
Acton
93
Dorfold Hall
NBCYC
aqueduct
92
36
River Weaver
Nantwich
school

NANTWICH BASIN
stop gate
92
70'
Nantwich Canal Centre
Simolda

mus
Safeway

A530 to Whitchurch   A51 to Stone
A530 to Middlewich

HURLESTON and Barbridge are the 'Clapham Junctions' of the inland waterways. Throughout the cruising season the section between them is often frenetic with boats converging and diverging to and from all points of the canal compass. Providentially the old Chester Canal (opened in 1779) was built to barge dimensions and there is usually plenty of room to manoeuvre. The Cheshire Plain's recurring image of spacious pastures grazed by Friesian cattle continues unabated; come milking time the herds shuffle udder-heavy across the accommodation bridges of the canal.

HURLESTON JUNCTION, with its quartet of locks, is the starting point of the Llangollen Canal's serene journey into Wales; a route fully covered in our *Welsh Waters Canal Companion*. It's overlooked by a high-banked reservoir which receives its water supplies from the Llangollen Canal, a factor instrumental in the survival of the waterway back in 1944 when there were proposals to close it.

BARBRIDGE JUNCTION marks the beginning and end of the Middlewich Branch of the Shropshire Union Canal, and it is, along with Middlewich, Great Haywood and Autherley, a pivotal point for all Four Counties Ring travellers. On this map we include the length of canal up to Bunbury simply for the benefit of boaters journeying to or from the boatyard there. Notwithstanding the A51's thundering traffic, Barbridge is a popular overnight mooring spot, with two pubs vying for custom. And there's the interest of the junction itself, where once a transhipment shed spanned the main line. You can detect its site where the canal narrows just south of the junction.

Summary of Facilities

Both the OLDE BARBRIDGE INN (Tel: 01270 528443), Bridge 100, and the JOLLY TAR (Tel: 01270 528283), opposite the junction, cater for families, offer a wide choice of food and have large gardens. Just beneath the embankment at Barbridge Junction the POST OFFICE STORES also deals in canal souvenirs. BUSES run from stops at Wardle linking Chester and Hanley via Nantwich. Tel: 01270 505350.

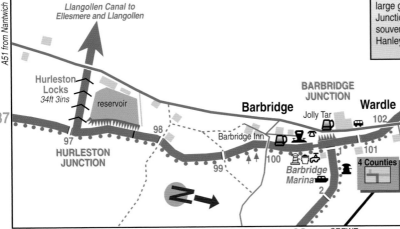

It's dispiriting to see how the Middlewich Branch towpath has been allowed to deteriorate after extensive refurbishment in the early 1990s. Why bother with improvements unless they can be maintained? Budgets slashed one imagines!

REMOTE, and seemingly always windswept, the Middlewich Branch of the Shropshire Union cuts across the grain of the landscape on a series of high embankments. It can be a busy length of canal for, as well as Four Counties Ring traffic, it funnels boats to and from the hugely popular Llangollen Canal, consequently its four deep and heavy-gated locks can become bottlenecks at the beginning and end of summer weeks.

Historically, the branch, opened in 1833, belonged to the Chester Canal Company and was engineered by Thomas Telford. Trade was heavy in cargo-carrying days, as after opening of the Birmingham & Liverpool Junction Canal this became the optimum route between the Black Country and the industrial North-west. Trade also developed between Ellesmere Port on the banks of the Mersey and The Potteries: Cornish china clay in one direction, finished crockery in the other. In 1888 a curious experiment was undertaken, to see if it was feasible to replace horse-power by laying a narrow gauge railway along the towpath below Cholmondeston Lock, and employing a small steam locomotive called 'Dickie' to haul strings of narrowboats. The concept didn't develop here, laying track was considered cost-prohibitive and there were problems in steering the boats,

though it did catch on abroad, especially on the French waterways. Cholmondeston still retains a railway presence, however, in the shape of the Crewe to Chester line, part of the historic route of the Irish Mails to Holyhead.

A high wooded embankment carries the canal across the River Weaver. Four Counties Ring travellers meet the river again near Audlem. It rises on the south-facing slopes of the Peckforton Hills and passes beneath the Llangollen Canal at Wrenbury prior to becoming navigable at Winsford, less than five miles downstream of the Weaver Aqueduct. There is nothing spectacular about the canal's crossing of the river, but it takes place in the most agreeable of locations. And, as you pass on your elevated way, it's hard to escape a fleeting sense of regret that the riverbank, being on private land, cannot so easily be explored. A yearning, one suspects, for the unattainable: like the woman who drives past you every morning on the way to work but whom you will never get to know, or the job that you suspect you could do brilliantly but are unlikely to be ever offered.

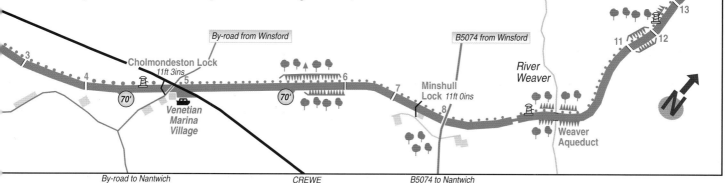

Church Minshull, Middlewich Branch

TO subconsciously relegate the Middlewich Branch to the back of your mind as an unspectacular, but necessary link in the waterways of the North-West would be unjust, for this is a rumbustious canal, extrovertly ushering you loftily above the snaking valley of the Weaver, presenting you with expansive views towards a horizon bounded by Delamere Forest and the Peckforton Hills. Church Minshull - all russet coloured brick and black & white half timbering - looks, from the canal's elevated position, like a toy village embracing the river's luxuriant banks. Tom and Angela Rolt enjoyed an extended stay here in the fateful Autumn of 1939 while Tom worked for Rolls Royce at Crewe. It was tedious work he didn't enjoy, but the couple revelled in the close-knit community which flourished at Minshull: the blacksmith who shod the local cart horses; and the miller whose water wheels supplied the village with its electricity, continuing to do so right up until 1960.

Several sizeable farms border the canal, their fields filled with dairy herds or cut red by the plough in a ruddy shade of corduroy. Near Bridge 22, woods partially obscure the Top Flash, a subsidence induced lake beside the Weaver. The main London-Glasgow railway crosses the canal, its sleek electric trains swishing by at thirty times the speed of your boat. To the south-east lies a forgotten, older transport route, a Roman road which linked the early salt mines at Nantwich and Middlewich. Some interesting old canal horse stables are being restored by Bridge 18.

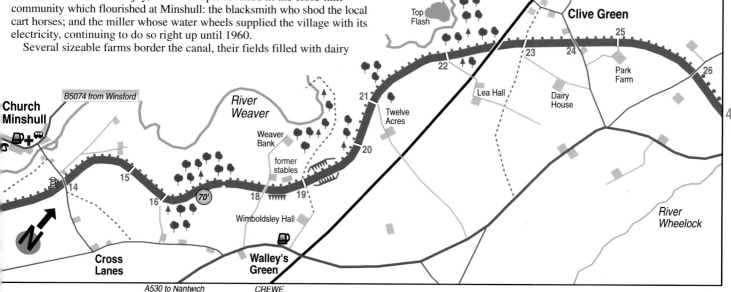

RUNNING through the upper valley of the Trent, a narrow, lacklustre stream difficult to equate with the river that this guide encounters at Derwentmouth, the Caldon Canal struggles to extricate itself from the urbanisation of The Potteries. When fields do finally appear they seem shaggy and unkempt, as though this were a no-man's-land between true countryside and town. Near Milton a short arm once led to Ford Green ironworks and Smallthorne Colliery, both vanished. Engine Lock, recalling the existence of a pumping engine in the vicinity of Cockshead Colliery, stands adjacent to a large works manufacturing porcelain insulators. At Norton Green the Knypersley Feeder (long ago navigable to a remote colliery basin) joins the canal. Knypersley is one of three reservoirs, along with Stanley and Rudyard, which feed into the Caldon, and thence the Trent & Mersey. The fledgling Trent is piped beneath the canal by Bridge 22. The Stockton Brook flight carries the canal forty feet up to its summit level of 486ft. Stone walls and small holdings begin to create a Pennine sense of obduracy.

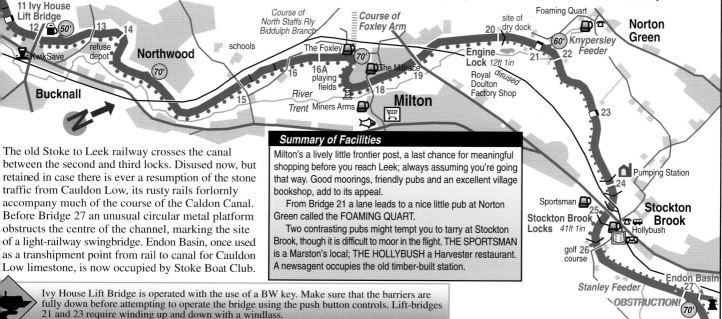

The old Stoke to Leek railway crosses the canal between the second and third locks. Disused now, but retained in case there is ever a resumption of the stone traffic from Cauldon Low, its rusty rails forlornly accompany much of the course of the Caldon Canal. Before Bridge 27 an unusual circular metal platform obstructs the centre of the channel, marking the site of a light-railway swingbridge. Endon Basin, once used as a transhipment point from rail to canal for Cauldon Low limestone, is now occupied by Stoke Boat Club.

Summary of Facilities

Milton's a lively little frontier post, a last chance for meaningful shopping before you reach Leek; always assuming you're going that way. Good moorings, friendly pubs and an excellent village bookshop, add to its appeal.

From Bridge 21 a lane leads to a nice little pub at Norton Green called the FOAMING QUART.

Two contrasting pubs might tempt you to tarry at Stockton Brook, though it is difficult to moor in the flight. THE SPORTSMAN is a Marston's local; THE HOLLYBUSH a Harvester restaurant. A newsagent occupies the old timber-built station.

Ivy House Lift Bridge is operated with the use of a BW key. Make sure that the barriers are fully down before attempting to operate the bridge using the push button controls. Lift-bridges 21 and 23 require winding up and down with a windlass.

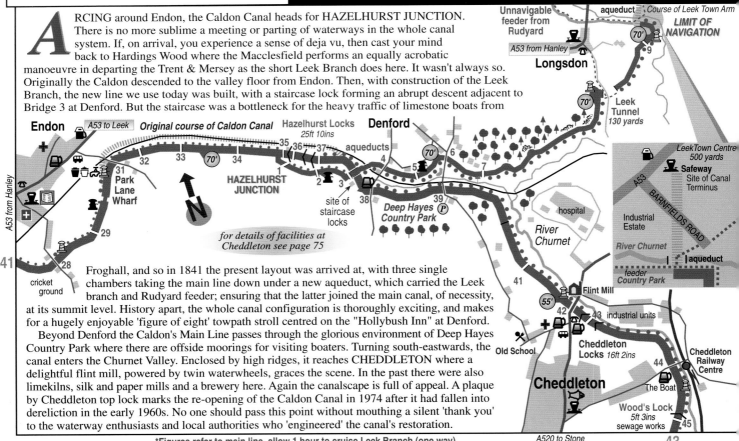

ARCING around Endon, the Caldon Canal heads for HAZELHURST JUNCTION. There is no more sublime a meeting or parting of waterways in the whole canal system. If, on arrival, you experience a sense of deja vu, then cast your mind back to Hardings Wood where the Macclesfield performs an equally acrobatic manoeuvre in departing the Trent & Mersey as the short Leek Branch does here. It wasn't always so. Originally the Caldon descended to the valley floor from Endon. Then, with construction of the Leek Branch, the new line we use today was built, with a staircase lock forming an abrupt descent adjacent to Bridge 3 at Denford. But the staircase was a bottleneck for the heavy traffic of limestone boats from

Froghall, and so in 1841 the present layout was arrived at, with three single chambers taking the main line down under a new aqueduct, which carried the Leek branch and Rudyard feeder; ensuring that the latter joined the main canal, of necessity, at its summit level. History apart, the whole canal configuration is thoroughly exciting, and makes for a hugely enjoyable 'figure of eight' towpath stroll centred on the "Hollybush Inn" at Denford.

Beyond Denford the Caldon's Main Line passes through the glorious environment of Deep Hayes Country Park where there are offside moorings for visiting boaters. Turning south-eastwards, the canal enters the Churnet Valley. Enclosed by high ridges, it reaches CHEDDLETON where a delightful flint mill, powered by twin waterwheels, graces the scene. In the past there were also limekilns, silk and paper mills and a brewery here. Again the canalscape is full of appeal. A plaque by Cheddleton top lock marks the re-opening of the Caldon Canal in 1974 after it had fallen into dereliction in the early 1960s. No one should pass this point without mouthing a silent 'thank you' to the waterway enthusiasts and local authorities who 'engineered' the canal's restoration.

*Figures refer to main line, allow 1 hour to cruise Leek Branch (one way).

for details of facilities at Cheddleton see page 75

43

The Leek Arm

From Hazelhurst, the branch to Leek curves away from the main line which locks attractively down to pass beneath it. Two overbridges precede a sharp turn at the site of the old staircase locks before the branch then crosses the main line on an imposing brick aqueduct (pictured on our title page) dated 1841. A lesser aqueduct over the railway follows before the branch settles down on the opposite hillside for the delightful journey to Leek. Winding, dipping in and out of overbridges, and passing some envy-provoking waterside properties, the canal traverses a gorgeous belt of woodland, full of bluebells in spring, where jays screech mockingly amongst the tree tops and brackeny banks spill down into the valley of the River Churnet. Presently the view ahead opens out towards the high flanks of The Morridge rising to 1,300ft in the east, whilst glowering over your right-hand shoulder stands the spooky tower of Leekbrook Asylum. If the inmates weren't deranged before they were incarcerated here, they would probably be sent mad by the sheer despondency of the hospital's grim institutional architecture.

All of a sudden the canal encounters a remote pool enclosed by lowhills - one of the most idyllic mooring spots on the whole system. The canal builders had no alternative but to dig a tunnel in order to reach Leek. The confined 130 yard bore is fronted by an ornate portal of red sandstone. Walkers take the horsepath across the top and are rewarded by stunning views over the town to the The Roaches beyond.

Less than a mile of canal remains in water. The final turning point for all but the smallest cabin cruiser is just beyond Bridge 9. Around the corner the canal peters out as its feeder comes in from Rudyard, three miles to the north. A public footpath (part of the "Staffordshire Way") follows the feeder to the reservoir which gave us Kipling's christian name. An aqueduct, dated 1801, once carried the canal across the Churnet to reach a terminal wharf nearer the town centre. The aqueduct remains but is bereft of water, whilst the bed of the canal lies beneath an industrial estate. A sad loss to this now tourist-conscious town, although the creation of a country park here has done much to enhance the setting of the current terminus.

Leek

A vigorous town of looming textile mills, gaunt Victorian architecture and some still cobbled streets, Leek is tucked away from the outside world in deep folds of the Staffordshire Moorlands, conforming to everyone's mental image of a typical northern mill town. In fact it is an entertaining and evocative place to explore, and canal travellers are entitled to mourn the disappearance of the old terminal arm and the resultant bleak trudge through an industrial estate which forms their initial, and definitely misleading, impression of Leek.

GREYSTONES - Stockwell Street. Absolutely brilliant tearooms in 17th century house. Tel: 01538 398522.

DEN ENGEL - St Edwards Street. Tel: 01538 373751. Little Belgium comes to North Staffs. Great fun! *Lots of pubs, fish & chips, Baltis etc elsewhere in the town.*

 All facilities can be found in the town centre a mile north-east of the canal, though there is a large SAFEWAY store nearer at hand. The outdoor market is held on Wednesday and Saturdays, but the charming little indoor market also functions on Fridays, whilst Thursday is half-day. The delight of shopping in Leek lies in the proliferation of small shops offering individuality and personal service. Regular CC users will know that each revisit to Leek involves a heart-in-the-mouth pilgrimage to St Edward's Street to see that PICKFORDS divinely unspoilt grocery store still functions. Devastatingly, on this occasion, we discovered an empty shell: the glorious tiled walls still gleaming, but no longer any tins stacked in pyramids on the counter, or trays of fresh vegetables laid out on the pavement to lure you in to be tempted by all manner of delicacies. This loss all the more personally poignant since we had interviewed Mr and Mrs Pickford earlier in the year for another publishing project. They'd had no doubt then that the supermarkets would eventually 'do' for them, and how sadly right their pessimism proved. Mourn the loss of another traditional shop and console yourself with some fresh oatcakes and pikelets from ASPLINS on Haywood Street. Lindsay Asplin's grandparents started making oatcakes here forty years ago, and they're still freshly prepared daily to the same highly secret recipe. More modern in outlook, but still charming, is COUNTRY CUISINE in Sheepmarket Street, a friendly delicatessen and bakery. There's an excellent secondhand bookshop on Stockwell Street whilst Leek is enjoying a burgeoning reputation as a centre for antiques.

A number of the textile mills operate factory shops selling their products direct to the public and information about these is available from the Tourist Information Centre.

TOURIST INFORMATION CENTRE - Market Place. Tel: 01538 483741.

BRINDLEY MILL/JAMES BRINDLEY MUSEUM - Mill Street. Small admission charge. Tel: 01538 399332. Open Easter- September Sat, Sun & BH Mons 2-5pm. Open same hours Mons, Tues & Weds in late July/August. Restored water powered corn mill built by James Brindley in 1752.

BUSES - frequent service to/from Hanley and connections with Cheddleton and Froghall. Tel: 01782 207999.

Idyllic moorings - Leek Tunnel pool

erry Eye Bridge

Consall Forge - trains, boats, but *no* cars!

BEYOND Cheddleton the enchantment deepens as the Caldon engenders an almost Amazonian sense of solitude. Briefly, in a distant echo of the arrangement at Alrewas (Map 16) the canal merges with the River Churnet at OAKMEADOW FORD LOCK, though there is little change of character, other than when heavy rainfall causes the river current to increase its normally sluggish pace.

You begin to wonder why on earth they ever bothered to build a canal in such an extraordinarily remote outpost of Staffordshire. But this is a countryside with plenty of skeletons in its closet. Haematite iron ore and limestone were extensively mined in the area, and there were also several coal shafts and flint-grinding mills. At its zenith in the 1860s, an average of thirty boats a day were carrying ore out of the Churnet Valley.

The Caldon Canal was promoted for two main reasons: for the export of limestone from Cauldon Low; and to provide the summit of the Trent & Mersey with extra water. It opened in 1779, but was literally the death of James Brindley, who caught pneumonia on a surveying trip with fatal consequences for that genius of the early canal era.

Reaching CONSALL FORGE, the river disengages itself from the canal, disappearing over a weir to race ahead down the valley. The canal, however, makes light of this snub, passing under the railway, once a picturesque byway of the North Staffordshire Railway, now a preserved steam line. The channel grows noticeably more slender, so that the passing of oncoming boats becomes a matter of discretion and a little 'give and take'. Squeezing past the old cantilevered waiting room of Consall station, the canal descends through the deep FLINT MILL LOCK, passes Consall Mill, and twists round the valley to the distinctively arched Cherry Eye bridge recalling, it is said, the inflamed, bloodshot eyes of the neighbourhood's ironstone workers.

A newly concreted section of canal follows as an embanked length prone to breaching is negotiated. Woodland tumbles down to the water's edge on one side, whilst on the other, an equally steep descent leads to the river. Suddenly a factory wall looms out of the trees, heralding the vast copper wire works of Thomas Bolton & Sons. The factory dates from 1890 and once operated a small fleet of narrowboats, though most of its transport needs were supplied by the railway. It was turned over to munitions during the war and apparently the Luftwaffe tried to bomb it but couldn't find it; which is not surprising when you take into account its position in this amphitheatre of heavily wooded hills.

Journey's end is frustratingly foreshortened for all but a few boaters by

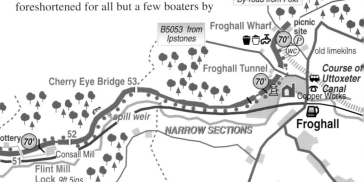

the restricted bore of Froghall Tunnel. A winding hole is provided by the copper works. If, however, your boat is one of the few that conforms to the tunnel's loading gauge you can proceed to the picturesque terminal which lies beyond it. The rest of us must follow the path around the side.

The peace and quiet of FROGHALL BASIN today is hard to reconcile with the busy basin where limestone, brought down by plate tramway from the quarries, was cut to size and loaded on to narrowboats. Here were sidings, great banks of limestone, smoking kilns, and, significantly, the top lock of the Uttoxeter extension, the site of which can still be discerned at the apex of the winding hole. But over seventy-five years have passed since the wharf was abandoned commercially, and in the intervening period nature has reclaimed her own. A picnic site is now located in the shadow of the lime kilns and a trip boat operates from the old wharf building. Several signposted walks can be enjoyed in the vicinity, or you can just laze by the canal, soaking in the setting's remarkable feeling of calm whilst marvelling at the fragility of time.

Queuing for ice cream - Froghall Wharf

Cheddleton (Map 42)

Interesting village (St Edward's church has some fine Pre-Raphaelite stained glass) offering shopping and refreshment opportunities before you head into the interior. There are two small supermarkets half a mile up the hill from the canal, and a post office by Bridge 42. Three pubs, including the charming BOAT INN (Tel: 01538 360683) by Bridge 44, compete for your custom. There's a fish & chip shop too, but we were most impressed by THE OLD SCHOOL TEA ROOM AND CRAFT SHOP (Tel: 01538 360521) in Hollow Lane - scrummy home made cakes!
CHEDDLETON FLINT MILL - open weekend afternoons. One of the great little museums of England.
CHURNET VALLEY RAILWAY - operates Sats, Suns, some Summer Weds & Bank Hol Mons. Tel: 01538 360522. Preserved steam railway slowly extending through the valley, probably running as far as Froghall by the time you read this. Much nostalgia plus an excellent way to facilitate a one-way towpath walk.
BUSES - services to/from Leek and Hanley also useful for towpath walks. Tel: 01785 207999.

Consall Forge

Peace and tranquillity characterise Consall to such an extent now that it is hard to visualise the activity of the forges, furnaces and slitting mills which clustered here in the seventeenth and eighteenth centuries. Now, though, it is for the isolated BLACK LION (Tel: 01782 550294) that Consall Forge is best known. A tad more 'worldy wise' than of yore, yet still one of the most delightful pubs on the inland waterway system, it offers Marston's ale and an good range of meals which may be enjoyed either in the cosy interior or the spacious garden where you can watch the boats and the steam trains go gaily by. Just a stroll away is CONSALL NATURE PARK and the recently opened station on the Churnet Valley Railway.

Froghall

The 'village' consists almost entirely of the copper wire works, yet oddly enough this does not compromise the sense of isolation which pervades the otherwise unspoilt valley of the Churnet. The RAILWAY HOTEL (Tel: 01538 754782) is a Marston's pub serving bar meals (Thurs-Mon) but there are no shops of any kind in Froghall. Buses offer a handy service for towpath walkers.Tel: 01782 207999. The trip boat operates public excursions on Thursday mornings and Sunday afternoons throughout the summer months, as well as being available for private charter. Tel: 01538 266486. Ice creams and drinks are often available from the wharf house. Some newly built self-catering cottages are available for let by the canal terminus - Tel: 01538 266160.

How to use the Maps

There are forty-three numbered maps. Maps 1 to 22 cover the Trent & Mersey Canal in its entirety from Preston Brook to Derwentmouth; Maps 13 and 23 to 27 cover the northern half of the Staffordshire & Worcestershire Canal; and Maps 27 to 40 cover the Shropshire Union from Autherley via Barbridge to Middlewich. The Caldon Canal, a branch of the Trent & Mersey, appears on Maps 8 and 41 to 43. Boaters navigating the FOUR COUNTIES RING should use Maps 4 to 13, and 27 to 40. Travelling clockwise around the ring - no matter where you start - from read the maps from left to right; anti-clockwise, right to left. For example, if you were to cruise the whole of the ring from Brewood in an anti-clockwise direction, you would turn first to Map 28 then 27, etc to 23; then 13, 12, 11 etc to 4; then 40, 39 etc back to 28. In any case the simplest way of proceeding from map to map is to turn to the next map numbered from the edge of the map you are on. Figures quoted at the top of each map refer to distance per map, locks per map and average cruising times. An alternative indication of timings from centre to centre can be found on the Route Planner inside the front cover. Obviously cruising times vary with the nature of your boat and the number of crew at your disposal, so quoted times should be taken only as an estimate. Neither do times quoted take into account any delays which might occur at lock flights in the high season.

Using the Text

Each map is accompanied by a route commentary describing the landscape and placing the canal in its historic context. Details of most settlements passed through are given together with itemised or summarised information of facilities likely to be of interest to canal users.

Eating & Drinking: Under this category we indicate a selection of establishments likely to be of use to users of the guide. We don't set out to make judgements in an Egon Ronay sense, but, generally speaking, the more detail we give, the more impressed we were with the place in question. It is desperately difficult to keep pace with changes at pubs and restaurants in particular, and we apologise in advance for any entries in the text subsequently overtaken by events.

Shopping in strange towns and villages is one of the great pleasures of canal travel. Under this category we try to outline the basic facilities for shopping in any given location as well as mentioning any especially interesting, unusual, quirky, charming, or simply timeless shops worth patronising for the experience alone.

Places to Visit: This is the age of the 'one-third A4 tourist attraction leaflet' and you may already possess material appertaining to every visitor centre within 50 miles radius of your itinerary. Nevertheless, we wouldn't be doing our job properly if we didn't outline attractions within easy reach of the canal, many of which seem all the more enjoyable when visited by boat.

Public Transport: Information in this category is quoted especially with the use of towpath walkers in mind, making 'one-way' walks using bus or train in the opposite direction. However we urge you to check with the telephone number quoted to ascertain up to the minute details of timetables etc.

Towpath Walking

After years of official neglect and indifference, numerous towpath improvement schemes have re-awakened public enthusiasm for walking beside canals. As an aid to walkers the maps in this guide depict the towpath in three categories. GOOD can usually be taken to indicate the existence of a firm, wide, dry base suitable for comfortable walking and cycling; ADEQUATE hints at the chance of mud and vegetation, but can usually be considered passable; whilst POOR speaks for itself - diehards may get through, but it won't be much fun. By and large the towpaths of the Four Counties Ring are in good condition. The worst stretch is probably that north of Hack Green Locks on the Shropshire Union Canal and even there progress is possible with perseverance.

Towpath Cycling

Cycling canal towpaths is an increasingly popular activity, but one which British Waterways - the body responsible for the upkeep of the bulk of Britain's navigable inland waterways - is only slowly coming to terms with. At present it is necessary for cyclists wishing to use towpaths to acquire a free of charge permit from a British Waterways office - see opposite.

Boating

Boating on inland waterways is an established, though relatively small, facet of the UK holiday industry. There are over 20,000 privately owned boats registered on the canals, but in addition to these, numerous firms offer boats for hire. These range from small operators with half a dozen boats to sizeable fleets run by companies with several bases.

Traditionally, hire boats are booked out by the week or fortnight, though many firms now offer more flexible short breaks or extended weeks. All reputable hire firms give newcomers tuition in boat handling and lock working, and first-timers soon find themselves adapting to the pace of things.

Navigational Advice

Locks are part of the charm of canal cruising, but they are potentially dangerous environments for children, pets and careless adults. Use of them should be methodical and unhurried, whilst special care should be exercised in rain, frost and snow when slippery hazards abound. The majority of locks featured in this guide are of the narrow variety, but on the Trent & Mersey *east* of Burton-on-Trent they are widebeam and can fit two narrowboats side by side.

Mooring on the canals featured in this guide is as per usual - ie on the towpath side, away from sharp bends, bridge-holes and narrows. Recommended moorings, of particular relevance to urban areas, are marked on the maps with an open bollard symbol. Long term moorings, usually requiring a permit, are indicated with a closed bollard symbol. Remember always to slow down when passing moored craft.

Closures - known as 'stoppages' on the canals - usually occur between November and April when maintenance work is undertaken. Occasionally, however, an emergency stoppage may be imposed at short notice. Up to date details are usually available from hire bases. British Waterways provide a recorded message service for private boaters. The number to ring is: 01923 201401. Stoppages are also listed on BW's internet web site at www.british-waterways.org

Harecastle Tunnel - a timetable of entry periods operates through the 'single-lane' tunnel at Harecastle on Map 7. In the interest of safety the tunnel is only open when manned by the tunnel-keepers who have offices adjacent to the north and south portals of the tunnel. Operating times are as follows:
WINTER HOURS - November to mid-March. The tunnel is only open by appointment (Mon-Sat). Telephone 01782 785703 giving at least 48 hours notice.
NORMAL HOURS - Mid March to mid May and mid September to end October. The tunnel is open for passage between 8am and 5pm. *To be guaranteed a passage craft must arrive by 3pm.*
SUMMER HOURS - Mid-May to Mid-September. As above but open until 6pm. *For last guaranteed passage arrive by 4pm.*

Caldon Canal - beyond Cheddleton the Caldon Canal merges briefly with the River Churnet. At Oakmeadowford Lock a gauge indicates water safety levels and boaters are advised not to enter the river if the water level is over the six inch mark. Froghall Tunnel is extremely restricted in width and height and most boats are unlikely to be able to squeeze through. A 70 foot winding hole (just!) now exists by the Copper Works on the Hazelhurst side of the tunnel, whilst *if* you are able to pass through the tunnel another full length winding hole is located at Froghall Wharf.

Emergencies

British Waterways operate a central emergency telephone service. Dial the operator and ask for FREEPHONE CANALS. For mobile users the number is 01384 215785.

British Waterways Contacts

Peak & Potteries Trent & Mersey Canal north of Trentham and Caldon Canal - Red Bull Wharf, Congleton Road South, Kidsgrove, Stoke-on-Trent ST7 3AP. Tel: 01782 785703.
Fradley Junction Trent & Mersey Canal south of Colwich - Fradley Junction, Burton-on-Trent DE13 7DN. Tel: 01283 790236.
Norbury Junction Staffs & Worcs Canal, Trent & Mersey Canal Trentham to Colwich and Shropshire Union Canal south of Audlem - Norbury Junction, Stafford ST20 0PN. Tel: 01785 284253.
Border Counties Shropshire Union Canal north of Audlem including the Middlewich Arm - Wharfside, Chester CH1 4EZ Tel: 01244 390372.

Societies

The Inland Waterways Association was founded in 1946 to campaign for retention of the canal system. Many routes now open to pleasure boaters may not have been so but for this organisation. Membership details may be obtained from: Inland Waterways Association, PO Box 114, Rickmansworth WD3 1ZY. Tel: 01923 711114. Fax 01923 897000.

Web Sites

George's Canal Boating: www.canals.com
British Waterways: www.british-waterways.org
Pearsons Canal companions: www.jmpearson.co.uk

Acknowledgements

Monster thanks to all involved: Brian Collings - we're *pretty* sure that this is his *thirtieth* signwritten cover for us so far!; to all at Graphic Solutions; to Toby Bryant; to BW at Red Bull; to all our correspondents; and to Jackie and Karen for all those pub lunches in the name of research.

Information 2

Boating Facilities

Hire Bases

ALVECHURCH BOAT CENTRES - Trent & Mersey Canal Map 2. Scarfield Wharf, Alvechurch, Worcestershire B48 7SQ. Tel: 0121-445 2909. Fax: 0121-447 7120. www.alvechurch.com

ANDERSEN BOATS - Trent & Mersey Map 4. Wych House, Lewin Street, Middlewich CW10 9QB.Tel: 01606 833668.

ANGLO WELSH WATERWAY HOLIDAYS - Trent & Mersey Canal Map 13 and Shropshire Union Canal Maps 29 & 38. 5 Portland Place, Pritchard Street, Bristol BS2 8RH. Tel: 0117 9240332. Fax: 0117 9240202.

BLACK PRINCE HOLIDAYS - Trent & Mersey Canal Maps 1 & 8. Stoke Prior, Bromsgrove, Worcestershire B60 4LA. Tel: 01527 575115.

CANAL CRUISING - Trent & Mersey Canal Map 10. Crown Street, Stone ST15 8QN. Tel: 01785 813982.

CLAYMOORE NAVIGATION - Bridgewater Canal Map 1. The Wharf, Preston Brook, Warrington, Cheshire WA4 4BA. Tel: 01928 717273.

COUNTRYWIDE CRUISERS - Shropshire Union Canal Map 28. The Wharf, Brewood, Staffs ST19 9BG. Tel: 01902 850166.

JANNEL CRUISERS - Trent & Mersey Canal Map 18. Shobnall Marina, Burton-on-Trent DE14 2AU.Tel: 01283 542718.

MIDDLEWICH NARROWBOATS - Trent & Mersey Canal Map 4. Canal Terrace, Middlewich CW10 9BD. Tel: 01606 832460.

SIMOLDA - Shropshire Union Map 37. Basin End, Nantwich CW5 8LA. Tel: 01270 624075.

STAFFORDSHIRE NARROWBOATS - Trent & Mersey Canal Map 10. Newcastle Road, Stone ST15 8JW. Tel: 01785 816871.

SWAN LINE CRUISERS - Trent & Mersey Canal Map 16. Fradley Junction, Alrewas, Burton-on-Trent DE13 7DN. Tel: 01283 790332.

TEDDESLEY BOAT COMPANY - Staffs & Worcs Canal Map 24. Teddesley Road, Penkridge, Stafford ST19 5RH. Tel: 01785 714692. Fax: 01785 714894. www.narrowboats.co.uk

VIKING AFLOAT - Staffs & Worcs Canal Map 25. Lowesmoor Wharf, Worcester WR1 2RS. Tel: 01905 610660. Fax: 01905 616715. www.viking-afloat.com

WATER TRAVEL - Shropshire Union Canal Map 27. Oxley Moor Road, Wolverhampton WV9 5HW. Tel: 01902 782371.

Hire Agency

HOSEASONS HOLIDAYS Sunway House, Lowestoft, Suffolk NR32 2LW. Tel: 01502 501010. Fax: 01502 586781. www.hoseasons.co.uk

Other Boatyards

ANDERTON MARINA - Trent & Mersey Canal Map 2. Tel: 01606 79642.

ANGLO-WELSH - Trent & Mersey Canal Map 13 Tel: 01889 881711; Shropshire Union Canal Map 31 - Tel: 01785 284292; and Shropshire Union Canal Map 38 - Tel: 01829 260638.

BARBRIDGE MARINA - Shropshire Union Canal Map 38. Tel: 01270 528682.

BARNTON WHARF - Trent & Mersey Canal Map 2. Tel: 01606 783320.

BARTON TURN MARINA - Trent & Mersey Canal Map 17. Tel: 01283 711666.

CALF HEATH MARINA - Staffs & Worcs Canal Map 25.Tel: 01902 790570.

DOBSONS - Trent & Mersey Canal Map 22. Tel: 01332 792271.

DOLPHIN BOATS - Trent & Mersey Canal Map 8. Tel: 01782 849390.

ENGINEERING & CANAL SERVICES - Trent & Mersey Canal Map 12. Tel: 01889 882611.

HASSALL GREEN CANAL CENTRE - Trent & Mersey Canal Map 5. Tel: 01270 762266.

HATHERTON MARINA - Staffs & Worcs Canal Map 25. Tel: 01902 791887.

JD BOAT SERVICES - Staffs & Worcs Canal Map 31. Tel: 01902 791811.

KINGS LOCK CHANDLERY - Trent & Mersey Canal Map 4. Tel: 01606 737564.

LONGPORT WHARF - see Stoke-on-Trent Boatbuilding.

MARINE SERVICES - Trent & Mersey Canal Map 8. Tel: 01782 201981.

MIDLAND CANAL CENTRE - Trent & Mersey Canal Map 20. Tel: 01283 701933.

NANTWICH CANAL CENTRE - Shropshire Union Canal Map 37. Tel: 01270 625122.

ORCHARD MARINA - Trent & Mersey Canal Map 3. Tel: 01606 42082.

OTHERTON BOAT HAVEN - Staffs & Worcs Canal Map 24. Tel: 01785 712515.

RED BULL SERVICES - Trent & Mersey Map 6 Tel: 01782 779033.

SAWLEY MARINA - Trent Navigation Map 22. Tel: 0115 973 4278.

SHARDLOW MARINA - Trent Navigation Map 22. Tel: 01332 792832.

STOKE ON TRENT BOATBUILDING - Trent & Mersey Canal Map 7. Tel: 01782 813831.

STONE BOATBUILDING - Trent & Mersey Canal Map 10. Tel: 01785 812688.

TED'S BOATYARD - Shropshire Union Canal Map 34. Tel: 01630 658282.

TOM'S MOORINGS - Staffs & Worcs Canal Map 24. Tel: 01543 414808.

VENETIAN MARINA VILLAGE - Shropshire Union Canal Map 39. Tel: 01270 528318.

WINCHAM WHARF CANAL CENTRE - Trent & Mersey Canal Map 3. Tel: 01606 44672.

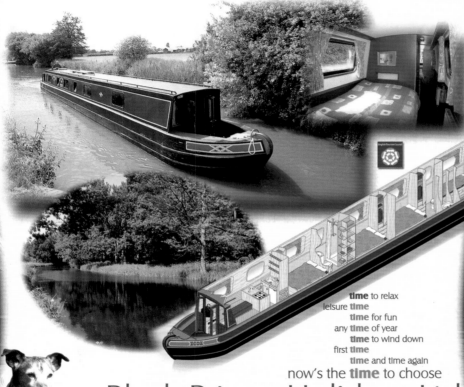

Waterways World

the *NUMBER ONE* inland waterways magazine

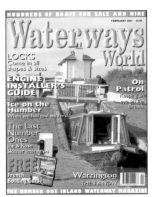

● **News** each month *Waterways World* reports all that is happening around the waterway system.

● **Canal heritage** restoration reports, waterway history - the boats, people and companies that worked and built the canal system.

● **Boat sales** more boats for sale every month than any other inland waterway magazine.

● **Practical advice** boat owners and aspiring boat owners - new and used narrow boat and cruiser reviews, engine development, and much more.

● **Enjoyment of the waterways** explore a different waterway each month with cruising reports, waterside walks, hire boat reviews, continental cruising.

Available from newsagents, boatyards and on subscription

Published by Waterways World Ltd, The Well House, High Street, Burton-on-Trent, Staffs DE14 1JQ. Telephone 01283 742970